Pra

ASPATORE

Aspatore Books, a Thomson Reuters business, exclusively publishes C-Level executives and partners from the world's most respected companies and law firms. Each publication provides professionals of all levels with proven business and legal intelligence from industry insiders—direct and unfiltered insight from those who know it best. Aspatore Books is committed to publishing an innovative line of business and legal titles that lay forth principles and offer insights that can have a direct financial impact on the reader's business objectives.

Each chapter in the *Inside the Minds* series offers thought leadership and expert analysis on an industry, profession, or topic, providing a future-oriented perspective and proven strategies for success. Each author has been selected based on their experience and C-Level standing within the business and legal communities. *Inside the Minds* was conceived to give a first-hand look into the leading minds of top business executives and lawyers worldwide, presenting an unprecedented collection of views on various industries and professions.

INSIDE THE MINDS

Building and Encouraging Law Firm Diversity

Leading Lawyers on Creating and Maintaining an Inclusive Firm Culture

2015 EDITION

ASPATORE

For additional copies or customer service inquiries, please e-mail west.customer.service@thomson.com.

ISBN 978-0-314-29394-7

Mat #41840403

CONTENTS

Diversity: An Essential Tool for Dealing with a Multicultural Marketplace

Fernando L. Roig

Founding Partner

ROIG Lawyers

ASPATORE

Introduction

Diversity is a key tool in the growth and prosperity of the legal profession. Increasing diversity in the legal market to mirror our diverse society is essential to growing and flourishing. Diversity will allow law firms to grow, and it will attract key clients necessary for progress. Progress and prosperity are linked to diversity since diversity cultivates a creative, effective, efficient, smarter, and better-equipped law firm.

Building a diverse law firm goes beyond simply hiring diverse attorneys. It requires a law firm to foster a cultural shift within the organization. Diversity allows you to provide your clients a fresh, dynamic variety of perspective ideas, and problem-solving strategies, all of which are beneficial in the service you are providing your clients.

Becoming Diverse

Law firms are defining diversity based on our diverse American society and their geographic locations. Our American society is a melting pot rich with diverse individuals and a culture the legal market has come to realize is essential in the progression of business. In today's legal climate, it is apparent that diversity is an integral part of the legal business as well as our societal fabric. As our American and global societies have expanded, blended, and grown over the past years, law firms have come to realize it is essential to absorb this change to be competitive. Many law firms are striving to be more diverse by implementing various programs such as committees, recruiting and mentoring programs, retention methods, and many other types of diversity initiatives.

Law firms continue to face various challenges in their pursuit to be at the forefront of diversity practices. One such challenge is creating an environment where differences are embraced and utilized creatively and not one that does not allow for growth or the opportunity to capitalize on the wealth of resources diverse attorneys bring to their business.

Another difficult challenge facing law firms is recruitment and retention of diverse attorneys. Law firms must address these challenges by increasing access to legal education for minority students. Aiding today's lawyers and law students to become tomorrow's legal leaders means a larger, more diverse marketplace and a greater pool of talented professionals. Recruiting professionals are instrumental in bridging the gap and aiding law firms in attaining diversity. Firms must continue to be vigilant to progress in these multicultural environments.

Attorneys in today's legal market are savvy when it comes to finding the right place to practice law. To retain talented, diverse attorneys, law firms often need to establish an innovative, modern, and cutting-edge legal practice, as well as a cohesive and inclusive culture. Mentorship programs help build such cultures, but one of the best steps law firms can take to create diversity is to simply hire more diverse attorneys: other attorneys will be attracted to firms that obviously value the insights and experience of people from different cultures and backgrounds. Law firms must recognize the value of different experiences, perspectives, and cultures, and must be committed to developing each individual attorney.

Law firms are benefiting from diversity immensely by hiring and retaining diverse attorneys. As a result, many within the profession are capitalizing on the benefits of this movement. Many clients, such as Fortune 500 corporations and small businesses, are requiring and seeking out law firms that are in line with their diversity initiatives. They are seeking attorneys with diverse backgrounds and continuously recruit law firms and attorneys to promote equity in legal opportunities through these initiatives. Law firms that are committed to diversity have a great understanding of various cultures and language skills, which allows them to cultivate business relationships throughout different networks. South Florida is a blueprint of legal diversity where diversity has allowed the legal profession to flourish financially and professionally. Various regions of the country can model South Florida's diversity efforts to ensure long-term survival through the ever-changing global economic climate.

Causes and Effects

The type of diversity clients prefer is not clear cut. Clients seek out a well-rounded mix of diversity. Today's clients prefer to hire legal counsel that is more of a reflection of their own corporate diversity and one that is in line with their corporate culture. That type of diversity is one that has women, African-Americans, Hispanic-Americans, Asian-Americans, and many more.

As society continues to grow and our culture is becoming ever more diverse, many clients have increased their expectations on the issue of diversity. For many of them, diversity is not an exception but the norm.

These large corporations will now look to law firms with the same scrutiny as they look to themselves regarding diversity. If law firms cannot measure up to their standards, many in the legal profession will be left behind. This is a great opportunity for the legal profession to take a look under the hood and determine if they are moving forward with regard to diversity or if they are still within a stagnant structure.

Diversity in the legal industry has always been discussed but never placed in the forefront of the profession. Legal professionals must address diversity now to align themselves with our global societies and global clients in the marketplace. Diverse clients are a key vehicle in opening the gateways to global business opportunities

It is estimated that by the year 2042, the population of the United States will be a "majority minority," and no one race or ethnicity will any longer be the majority in America. This key factor cannot be ignored by the legal community. The legal profession must adapt as soon as possible. We cannot turn a blind eye to this. Diversity in law firms should be a key priority in the recruiting process of talented professionals. Law firms should have a depth of cross-cultural understanding that allows them to communicate effectively when addressing the needs of diversity and changing client expectations in the global marketplace.

According to *The American Lawyer, "The Diversity Crisis," Diversity Scorecard 2014*, the number of minority lawyers who are not partners is at 19.5 percent. This statistic is very telling and very concerning for us as leaders in the legal profession. If it is estimated that our society will be a "majority minority" society and we do not reflect this within the legal industry, how will we continue to grow and prosper? How will clients look at us when deciding who they want to represent them?

The current economic climate is on an uptick, which should aid law firms in increasing diversity. During the hard times of the recession, many law firms scaled back many of their various initiatives and programs addressing diversity in the legal field. This scaling back has caused a stalemate in addressing diversity within our field. Now that the legal market is rebounding, law firms should begin or re-implement various initiatives needed to increase diversity.

Defining "Diverse"

Diversity is defined as the assemblage of a group of people who come from different walks of life, cultures, races, nationalities, experiences, and viewpoints. Diversity creates a law firm that is creative, effective, efficient, smarter, and better equipped in today's marketplace. This definition has arisen out of years of experience within the legal marketplace. As a Hispanic-American lawyer, I have experienced the legal profession as a minority firsthand, and I understand what diversity means.

Few areas in the United States are as diverse as South Florida. As a gateway to Latin America and the Caribbean, South Florida is home to multilingual and multiethnic cultures that enrich the global marketplace. Law firms must be adept at recognizing and capitalizing on the richness found in the diversity of their legal professionals, and they must understand that many of their firms' clients have a personal understanding of the economies and cultures of not only the principal nations of Latin America, but also the Caribbean Basin. There are an estimated 500 multinational headquarter corporations in Miami, many of which are here for the sole purpose of reaching these Latin markets.

The definition of diversity is a fluid one. We are constantly evolving as individuals, and as a result so does the definition of diversity. In the past few years, the definition has changed to encompass more than just race and nationality; now the meaning of "diversity" also includes an individual's personal experience. An individual's experience in life can range from the type of education one has received to how one deals with technology. Many of our younger attorneys are very tech savvy and are very much into the "millennial" culture. These young attorneys provide a depth of diversity to law firms through their personal experiences. The way they approach a problem and the methods used to solve it are very different from those that older attorneys at the firm use. This fresh viewpoint is a strength that every law firm can benefit from as we move toward the future.

The definition of diversity will never be stagnant, since we as a society are not stagnant. We are continuously evolving, growing, and experiencing new things that are directly related to all of us. This is inclusive of the legal profession, and we are not immune from the changes of the outside world.

Being Diverse

In today's increasingly multicultural global environment, a firm must recognize that the relative success of its clients' business interests depends, in great part, on the judgments and different experiences that can only be found in a diverse law firm. Being a diverse law firm has a number of benefits that range from a dynamic and creative work environment to a law firm that is nurturing and all-inclusive. Diversity helps make a law firm smarter, leads to better decisions, and helps in solving problems more effectively.

In dealing with diversity, there is not one particular type that is more beneficial than the other. Each type of diversity has its own specific and unique benefit that cannot be quantified. Building a diverse law firm, therefore, goes beyond simply hiring women and attorneys of color. It requires a law firm to cultivate a cultural shift within the organization, one that gives the same or greater priority to developing and retaining diverse attorneys once hired.

As legal professionals, we must consider the following factors when seeking to create a diverse law firm: the legal environment the firm is a part of, the type of cultures that have an impact on your business, and what your clients are looking for in terms of diversity. These factors are important, since they are essential in maintaining and building your client relationships and your revenue.

Many times, diversity lends itself to creating different avenues for business. If your firm is located within a large Hispanic-American population and many of your clients deal with South American/Central American regions, it would be imperative that your firm encompass what they are looking for, which would be Spanish-speaking legal counsel. These language skills allow for greater personal interaction with clients and expand abilities to serve clients in their native languages to address their unique legal needs. This form of diversity would be essential in building in a strong client relationship, which in turn would benefit the law firm financially.

Clients benefit enormously from a diverse law firm. You are able to provide your clients a fresh, dynamic variety of perspectives, ideas, problem-solving strategies, and creative work product, all of which are beneficial in the service you are providing to them. Law firms that do not embrace diversity will be stagnant and will offer the same type of work as all the other law firms out there in the market.

Changes

A law firm must not attempt things in a quick and haphazard manner. Before beginning any endeavor, the partners must engage in strategic planning and direction. This key step is essential to guide your law firm in the right direction. Law firm partners must lay out the goals they want to achieve and decide on the right direction to lead their firm to attain diversity.

Once strategic planning is completed, an initial step toward diversity is looking toward legal talent in the local marketplace. While gaining diverse legal talent, a law firm should also begin the infusion/inclusion of different cultural change from within. Law firms can create an inclusive culture that will allow them to build upon the strength of their diverse legal talent. This can be accomplished by establishing mentorship programs with senior attorneys and helping foster open lines of communication within the firm. Also, law firms can create an inclusive culture by providing all of its attorneys an open forum to share ideas and learn from one another that will help foster a diverse environment. All of these various endeavors should continue at a steady pace to create a strong foundation for diversity. Rapid and dramatic change will not lay down the foundation necessary to create fundamental change.

Conclusion

Be honest with yourself and your firm leaders. Assess your firm with open eyes, considering all the aspects of diversity, and recognize where it excels and where it can improve. Continue to evaluate both the firm and the market to set realistic diversity goals, and to continue being aware of diversity as your firm expands.

Being honest and realistic will allow you as a leader at your firm to identify and change the core issues and problems it may have regarding diversity. It will also allow you to identify your needs and find successful approaches to meet your diversity goals.

There are a number of useful resources out there to help managing partners reach their diversity goals, such as the American Bar Association, Minority Corporate Counsel, National Association for Law Placement, Hispanic Bar Association, Leadership Council on Legal Diversity, National Minority Supplier Development Council, Broward County Bar Association, Cuban American Bar Association, Gwen S. Cherry Black Women Lawyers Association, and Wilkie D. Ferguson Jr. Bar Association. Look to other firm leaders who have faced these issues and have achieved their diversity goals successfully. Finally, look to best practices or methods within other industries and how they have achieved their diversity goals.

Key Takeaways

- Consciously set about to become more diverse by implementing programs within the firm, such as recruiting and mentoring programs, retention methods, and other types of diversity initiatives suitable to your client base and location.
- Examine your methods for recruitment and retention of diverse attorneys. Consider increasing access to legal education for minority students, thereby making your marketplace wider and more diverse, with a greater pool of talented professionals.
- Create mentoring partnerships to ensure that all attorneys have a chance to progress in their careers at the firm.
- Be prepared for changes and encourage growth, because the definition of diversity is fluid.

Fernando L. Roig is the founding partner and co-chair of the executive committee of ROIG Lawyers. His innovative and transformative approach to law firm leadership has been instrumental in the firm's growth over the past decade. He has been influential in recruiting top-notch talent to the firm, which has expanded regionally to six offices across the state of Florida with more than 100 attorneys. The firm is recognized by the Daily Business Review *as the second most diverse law firm in South Florida and by the* South Florida Business Journal *as the seventeenth largest law firm in South Florida.*

Mr. Roig is known for being entrepreneurial and strategic with exceptional problem-solving, consensus-building, and negotiation skills, including an ability to structure and execute successful business tactics. Through his guidance, leadership, and vision, the firm successfully built new practice areas that have become drivers for the firm's overall success. He has long championed diversity and inclusion in business and the workplace, and he played a key role in creating and expanding advancement opportunities for women and minorities at the firm.

Mr. Roig brings more than twenty-five years of experience litigating insurance disputes and has guided clients toward the most efficient and inexpensive issue resolution, counseling them in ways to effectively avoid disputes and explore non-litigation alternatives such as mediation and arbitration. He has a proven record of success resolving large and complicated problems for clients, coordinating and defending high-stakes cases, and aggressively pursuing major recoveries for insurers. He has handled and tried hundreds of cases in federal and state courts.

Mr. Roig is an active leader in the legal community; he was selected by Governor Jeb Bush to serve on the Governor's Commission for the Everglades as well as the Fourth District Court of Appeals Judicial Nominating Committee. He is AV Preeminent peer review rated by Martindale-Hubbell and has been named to the 2015 South Florida Legal Guide *annual list as a "Top Lawyer" in commercial litigation.*

Diversity, Inclusiveness, and Firm Culture

Harry S. Johnson

Partner

Whiteford Taylor & Preston LLP

ASPATORE

Introduction

"Diversity" is a term that law firms across the country have embraced, but with little meaningful articulation of institutional cultural changes that will make the word more than a number-counting exercise. With few exceptions and with the recognition that demographics in a particular area may make recruitment difficult, most major markets have articulated that diversity is an important value. Statistics demonstrate that the number of diverse lawyers in major firms has remained essentially consistent. Women and certain ethnic groups are making progress, but the overall number of minority and women partners is not impressive. Retention and business development remain issues for diverse lawyers in even the most forward-thinking law firms.

In some areas, the number of available diverse lawyers makes it difficult to recruit. By way of example, a federal judge in rural Virginia told me several years ago that he would welcome having a minority law clerk. However, due to the lack of minorities in his community, young people were reluctant to go to a place where no one looked like them and they had no social outlets outside of work. He said he tended to hire married young law clerks that had their own family to interact with. This explanation is entirely rational, and it is not difficult to imagine that the same dynamic works in many smaller communities and firms. That same rationale has little resonance when speaking of any major firm in any major city in this country.

Defining Diversity

The word "diversity" means very little by itself. Diversity is number counting: how many people of different ethnicities or genders do we have in our firm? Number counting gives no evidence of the effort to provide meaningful opportunities to work and grow in a firm culture. To be truly diverse, a firm must have "inclusiveness" as one of its core values. Inclusiveness is having a seat at the table, whether that means hiring, work assignment, mentoring, client development, and/or firm management. If a firm does not establish, from top management, that the firm values inclusiveness as a core value, diversity is a meaningless shell.

Several legal publications have amassed statistics on diversity at law firms. In a 2014 survey of 223 firms, firms were ranked according to the percentage of minority attorneys in law firm jobs.[1] This survey focused specifically on African-American, Hispanic, and multiracial attorneys. It found that the number of minority attorneys in the reporting firms had increased slightly from 13.9 percent to 14.1 percent. The number of minority partners had also increased, to 7.6 percent from 7.3 percent the previous year. The survey found that Asian-American lawyers are the largest group of minority lawyers, at 6.3 percent, but only comprised 2.7 percent of firm partners. The number of Hispanic lawyers has also grown to a total of 3.2 percent, with 2.3 percent representing partners. The number of African-American attorneys was found to have decreased, so that they comprise only 1.9 percent of partners and 3.9 percent of overall attorneys. Not only was this the lowest overall percentage, but the survey found that this number had been slipping for the last five years.

The American Bar Association Commission on Women in the Profession annually publishes "A Current Glance at Women in the Law."[2] The 2014 glance shows that women comprise 20.2 percent of law firm partners and 17 percent of equity partners, while 44.8 percent of the firm associates are women. A similar figure is reflected in law school enrollment, where women are 47 percent of juris doctor candidates. This survey also reported that women comprise 27.1 percent of federal and state judgeships.

Inclusion and Economics

In many respects, law firms are no different than other businesses. They exist not only to provide quality services to their clients, but to generate revenue to support the lawyers, staff, and their families. Often, economics dictate firm policy. Economics impact diversity directly and harshly. Most major law firms have severely restricted or eliminated summer associate programs. These programs have traditionally been a vehicle that allowed second-year law students to work in a law firm environment, learn how a law firm operates, make relationships with "real lawyers," and earn a good salary for eight to twelve weeks. Over the past thirty years, this was the

---

[1] *Diversity Scorecard: How Firms Rate*, THE AMERICAN LAWYER (May 29, 2014), www.americanlawyer.com/id=1202657037862/Diversity-Scorecard-How-the-FirmsRate?slreturn=20150227162822.

[2] AMERICAN BAR ASSOCIATION COMMISSION ON WOMEN IN THE PROFESSION, A CURRENT GLANCE AT WOMEN IN THE LAW (2014), *available at* www.americanbar.org/content/dam/aba/marketing/women/current_glance_statistics_july2014.authcheckdam.pdf.

way an increasing number of women and ethnic minorities made their way into the associate ranks of firms. As the economy turned, so did the opportunity of both permanent employment and summer employment for diverse students. Some firms took the position that they did not want to have summer associates because they would not be able to offer them full-time employment if the student had a successful summer. This explanation is more of an economic excuse than a real concern. It would be difficult to find any second-year law student who would refuse the opportunity to work at a firm for a summer and get paid because they did not have the prospect of a full-time job after the summer. At the very least, the summer associate would make a salary and develop contacts, and hopefully have substantial written work product they could use to find permanent employment in the future.

Another way economics affect law firm diversity is the students themselves. The first issue is the cost of legal education. This factor influences all potential law students, but students from disadvantaged backgrounds may not find professional school to be a viable alternative. This is the "pipeline" issue that many in the profession, and in particular those in legal education, are trying to address. Second, for those who get into law school, we have seen the student debt rise to extraordinary levels. Law students graduate from school with staggering debt. With some firms delaying start dates or giving conditional employment offers, new lawyers may opt for non-law firm jobs that offer more certainty.

Responding to Client Needs and Values

Smart firms are responsive to client needs. A number of major corporations, through creative programs and collaborations with professional organizations like the American Corporate Counsel Association, Minority Corporate Counsel Association, American Bar Association Commission on Minorities in the Legal Profession, and National Bar Association Corporate Counsel Committee, have created programs that incentivize both in-house counsel and law firms to have diverse legal talent. The story of a major corporation that fired a major Midwest firm, after three years of requesting that the firm become more diverse, has become folklore. Firms must respond when clients ask about the demographics of the firm. When firms are asked to fill out surveys about the number of minority and women partners, some of them get the idea that the employing entities take diversity seriously.

Corporate boardrooms are evaluating the lack of diversity in America's law firms, even while some firms continue to ignore the emerging realities of a diverse and inclusive society. In an article published in the March 2015 American Corporate Counsel Association *Docket*, three board-level corporate leaders discuss *Fixing What's Broken: Strategies for Increasing Diversity in Law Firms*. The authors make many well-reasoned observations, including the following: "The mismatch between law firm demographics and those found in the leadership of client corporations, law schools, universities, and the general population promotes concerns that businesses will have to become more active in helping these firms understand that diversity is indispensable. Corporate achievement depends heavily on talent and teams. A high-performing company must look at the broadest possible talent pool for its attorneys, and this must include women and minorities. In addition, diversity plays a critical role in US law, where the decision makers (e.g., judges, juries, and regulators) reflect the general population, not the partnership makeup at large firms. It is fair to say that well over one out of every three matters that go to trial will be presided over by a woman or minority. Of the active federal judges, 32 percent are women and 23 percent are minorities, while 27 percent of the state court benches are woman and minority judges."

A persuasive case can easily be made that inclusive workforces are an economic engine for law firms. Local, city, and state governments provide substantial legal work, either representing government entities or representing and advising clients who must deal with them. Increasingly, these potential clients have minorities and/or women in decision-making roles. Does it make economic sense to respond to a government request for legal services with a team that does not reflect, at least in some part, the diversity of the employing entity? Those firms that do not understand this dynamic often do not, and should not, win the beauty contest. These decision makers are savvy. It is not good enough to have someone who fills a demographic who is not a contributing player on the team. Firms can no longer get away with the ploy that the James Mason character employed in the movie "The Verdict." The defense lawyer played by Mason was preparing with his all-white legal team for the cross-examination of the plaintiff's medical witness, who was an elderly African-American physician. After discussing the substantive defense strategy, Mason instructs his team to get that "African-American" associate to sit at the trial table. This transparent effort to give the appearance of diversity is, unfortunately, not as fictional as one might hope.

Expanding Qualifications and Reflecting Society

One of the biggest fallacies law firms perpetuate is that they cannot find qualified minority law students. The problem is in the word "qualified." The criteria used by many law firms eliminate most students, not just minority students. Women have fared better in this respect, because female law students are performing at the highest levels at all law schools. There are also minority students who are in the "top 10 percent" of class and "on law review." The problem is that those few students will get several interviews, but many firms will not look beyond those restrictive criteria. Suppose a firm widened the criteria to evaluate the "top 25 percent" rather than the "top 10 percent." It is very likely that more diverse candidates would fall into that group, and if given the opportunity to interview, be able to impress the hiring authority for the firm.

People of diverse backgrounds enrich a firm. All one has to do is view television commercials to see that America's corporations now see America as a diverse consuming public, with many ethnicities being represented in their advertising. Walk into almost any courthouse in this country and you will see diverse jurists presiding over the dockets. Now, more than sixty years after *Brown v. Board of Education of Topeka, Kansas*, diverse students can be found at all of the law schools in this country. No longer should legacy or country club relationships dictate hiring policy. Those firms that want to have a more diverse workforce can do so if they take steps to do so.

While certain corporate leaders are thinking about diversity, as evidenced above, America's boardrooms are still not diverse to a representative degree, and that lack of diversity causes law firms to not place diversity on the front burner. There are, however, a substantial number of companies that do have meaningful diversity on their boards, or diverse individuals as their chief executive officer, or general counsel. Some of these leaders have been influential in pushing the inclusiveness agenda. Even the more progressive of these leaders face an internal dilemma, however. Are they going to be the person who gives a "break the company" case to a minority lawyer who does not have a track record of working with that company? If the case goes bad, what type of second guessing will that person face within their company? Some progressive leaders have decided they are willing to take that chance. They recognize that talent is talent, and the color and the gender should not preclude talent from having opportunity.

Power and Control Considerations

Lastly, inclusion in a law firm setting is hard because it requires a conscious decision to give up power. Even more than firm management, partners who control substantial books of business make conscious decisions about who to give the choice assignments. More importantly, they make decisions about who to introduce to institutional clients. Law firm partners are not unlike other powerful people in society, in that they are reluctant to give up any portion of their power. In a law firm environment, there is no more powerful partner than the person who decides who gets to do the work. Unfortunately, too many partners who control business and work assignments do not put diversity into their calculation unless a client expresses a desire to have a diverse legal team. Staffing is also a problem for those few minority partners who have been successful in building a substantial book of business. A minority partner might be reasonably concerned about assigning only minority lawyers to his or her book of business. In so doing, the other lawyers in the firm might "pigeonhole" the minority lawyers and not select them to work on other projects. The lack of working with a variety of partners might then become an impediment to partnership for the younger lawyers.

In the end, inclusiveness is about opportunity. No one should advocate hiring a person only because they are of a certain ethnicity, color, or gender. True inclusiveness is about providing the work and contacts that are afforded to majority lawyers. Talent will rise to the top. Opportunity means providing situations where there is the need for hard work and the probability of success, but also providing an environment where failure to succeed is not automatically equated with a lack of competence or talent. At the end of the day, people should be given the opportunity to show their merit and what they bring to the table.

Embracing Opportunity

"As women and minorities who have enjoyed distinguished academic and professional careers continue to have significant influence as corporate counsel, it will become more unlikely they will hire law firms that cannot demonstrate they will remain relevant for a planning horizon that looks several decades into the future."[3]

The foregoing quote is the new reality. Many people who have traditionally risen to manage law firms come from a background where diversity was absent. Even those firms that have aggressively hired women and minorities find it difficult to nurture and retain those lawyers. A young lawyer without a firm mentor who is committed to that lawyer's success will find it very difficult to navigate the law firm world. Minority and women partners may want to mentor young lawyers, but must also generate business and provide excellent client service. Inclusiveness does not become an institutional culture unless and until management and the partnership decide it is important to the survival of the firm.

With the rise in minorities and women in decision-making positions, there is also a rise in the number of racial minorities and women in the leadership of law firms. As clients and demographics dictate, law firms that want to remain profitable will respond. In the past ten years, there have been an increasing number of women and minorities who have risen to the title of managing partner or chief executive officer of major law firms. Many firms have a chief diversity officer or diversity partner, and something that is called a Diversity Committee. In some firms, the Diversity Committee is comprised of only women and minority partners; in others, the committee represents all constituencies of the firm. These individuals are all excellent lawyers who have found a way to navigate not only preconceptions, but firm politics. The number is still few. Even those well-positioned partners can only be as effective as their partners are willing to allow them to be.

Suggestions and Tactics

There are several suggestions about what law firms can do to be more diverse and have an inclusive firm culture. The following list is not

---

[3] Mark Roellig et al., *Fixing What's Broken: Strategies for Increasing Diversity in Law Firms*, ASSOCIATION CORPORATE COUNSEL DOCKET, March, 2015, at 68.

exhaustive, but only a few ideas about how firms can move toward a more inclusive culture. First, law firms have the unique opportunity and obligation to change the culture of legal education. In its hiring practices, a firm can communicate to law placement offices that it wants to see a wider range of students than only the top 10 percent. With the intense pressure on law schools with regard to their placement statistics, there is a strong interest in working with law firms in this way. Even though the number of minority law students may be down from previous years, this still presents the best pool of new talent for law firms to employ and cultivate.

The partnerships with law schools do not have to be limited to candidates for permanent employment. Internship or clerkship programs that target diverse students benefit both the students and the firm. Students have the opportunity to be in the law firm environment, which in itself provides a valuable education. Firms have an opportunity to meet students when they have no pressure on them to make an employment decision. By so doing, a firm can benefit from exposure to young talent who are eager to learn.

This exposure can start before law school. Most local bar associations, as well as the American Bar Association, have pipeline programs that look to high school students who have an interest in law school. Likewise, most colleges have legal internship programs as part of their curriculum. Bringing diverse students into the firm through these programs will not only cast the law firm as a good corporate citizen, but will also have a positive impact on the firm culture. Many lawyers are amazed at how smart, astute, and motivated these young people prove to be.

Partnerships with government offices are also an opportunity to cultivate diverse talent. For the past few years in Maryland, several major law firms joined with the Office of the Attorney General to support a summer internship program for diverse students. The diverse students selected for this program came from across the country and were assigned to different areas in the agency. These same students, if they do not choose to go into government service, are potential employees for not only the supporting law firms, but for firms in their respective communities as well.

Another potential partnership opportunity for majority firms is partnership with minority-owned law firms. Some majority firms have entered into partnering arrangements with minority-owned firms, and this arrangement works on several levels. First, some government legal engagements require participation of a minority-owned business enterprise (MBE) or a women-owned business enterprise (WBE). Such partnerships give firms the opportunity to work with and develop relationships with minority and women lawyers. In turn, those law firms through their networks can provide contacts to other minority and women lawyers who might be a good fit for the majority law firm. Probably most importantly, working with lawyers who are not part of the firm structure allows the majority law firm lawyers to interact with quality people who are women or lawyers of color.

The firm needs to also look internally and ask itself the hard questions. If the firm has minority partners, are they ever candidates for major cases? Does the firm include minority and women lawyers in decisions about who gets work? Is firm management diverse? Is the firm supportive of business development efforts of women and minority lawyers, including financial support for minority and specialty bar associations or business groups? Does the firm compensation structure properly award and incentivize diverse lawyers? Does the firm select minority lawyers as practice group heads, or take them on client pitches?

One way to measure a firm's inclusion efforts is to take a look at their vendor relationships. Firms spend millions of dollars each year for supplies, catering, temporary employees, and other contractors. Where the law firm spends its money shows whether the firm has a genuine commitment to supporting a diverse firm and business community. An inclusive culture would create an atmosphere where minority and women vendors have a fair opportunity to provide their services to the firm. Encouraging and supporting diverse vendors sends a major message about the intentionality of a firm's culture in advancing inclusion.

Another way firms can promote inclusion is to celebrate intra-firm cultural or community events. Firm events can be planned around significant holidays or days of cultural significance, and be used as a community learning opportunity for the firm. By making these events firm-wide, both attorneys and staff can participate and feel "welcomed." Firms can also participate in community-directed initiatives that show a commitment to diversity. Whether supporting a clothing drive, a homeless person's representation project, legal assistance for military veterans, a shelter for abused spouses, or community home building projects, the firm can "do good" and promote a cultural value of inclusiveness.

Conclusion

"The life experience of all young lawyers entering the profession will immediately inform their judgments about opportunities for professional growth and fulfillment at the firms fostering inclusiveness versus those who do not."[4]

Law firms that do not embrace an inclusive culture risk damage to their future economic viability. This is work that requires intentionality and commitment. However, there is ample talent to allow firms to meet this challenge. The commitment must extend beyond hiring. Firms must decide how, in their own culture, to engage and support diverse lawyers and staff.

Diversity and inclusion committees are fine as far as they go, but the devil is in the details. A committee that is only made up of minority lawyers does not ultimately have the power to make meaningful changes in the firm culture. Absent the participation of majority partners who genuinely partner with their minority colleagues, the committee will constantly be rowing upstream. A true inclusion committee would include not only lawyers, but members of the staff as well. Firms can learn much from the opinions and participation of those who support our everyday success. Lawyers sometimes forget that the staff is as invested in serving clients as the lawyers. When we win a case, they savor the victory. When something goes the wrong way, they live through it with us. A committee that includes staff exhibits strongly that inclusiveness is a value of the firm and not merely lip service.

Ultimately, this should not be a painful exercise. Firms that have embraced inclusiveness have seen profit, both financially and in the culture of the firm. Such firms should be proud of their diversity. Having an inclusive culture is not only the "right" thing to do, but is also the economically and financially responsible way to grow and strengthen the firm. As more firms get "it,"

---

[4] *Id.*

those that do not will be left behind. With sound leadership in both the corporate and legal worlds, inclusiveness is a goal that all can seek to achieve.

Key Takeaways

- Look beyond statistics to nurture diversity in the firm by making inclusiveness a core value. This touches all areas and activities of the firm, such as hiring, work assignment, mentoring, client development, and firm management. From top management downward, establish that the firm values inclusiveness.

- Consider client needs, concerns, and values and assess the firm to make sure its components reflect the society it serves. Consider collaborating with professional organizations that incentivize acquiring diverse legal talent. Increasingly, potential clients have minorities and/or women in decision-making roles, and judges and opposing lawyers are more likely to be women and minorities. The decision makers in their cases will reflect the general population, not the partnership makeup of the firm. In terms of firm income, at the very least, common sense says the team providing legal services should reflect, at least in some part, the diversity of the employing entity, whether it is a corporation or the government.

- Overcome the hurdle of finding "qualified" minority law students by enlarging the criteria beyond the "top 10 percent," which in actuality eliminates most students, not just minorities. A better pool of diverse possibilities, while still providing "qualified" candidates, would be to evaluate the "top 25 percent."

- Focus on providing opportunity to achieve inclusiveness. The spotlight should not be on ethnicity, color, or gender, but providing the same work and contacts that go to majority lawyers. Talent will rise to the top. Opportunity means providing circumstances that need hard work, offer the chance for success, and where failure to succeed is not considered a proof of lack of competence or talent. Give everyone the opportunity to show their merit and what they can offer.

- Plan for future needs and client preferences by supporting mentoring of diverse lawyers within the firm. A young lawyer without a mentor committed to that lawyer's success will find it difficult to navigate the law firm world. Make it easier for minority and women partners to mentor young lawyers while generating business and providing excellent client service. Inclusiveness must become an institutional culture through management and the partnership deciding it is important to the survival of the firm and then acting on it.

Harry S. Johnson is a senior litigation partner at Whiteford Taylor & Preston LLP. He is a member of the Maryland and District of Columbia Bars. He graduated from the University of Maryland School of Law in 1979 and has practiced at his current firm since that time, becoming a partner in 1986. His practice concentrates on complex civil litigation, with a focus on mass tort litigation, products liability law, and business torts. He serves on the firm's Executive Board and has co-chaired the Ethics Committee for over twenty years. He has been recognized in Super Lawyers, Best Lawyers in America, *and* Chambers. *He is also active in civic and bar activities, serving as president of the Maryland State Bar Association from 2003 to 2004. He has been a member of the American Bar Association House of Delegates since 2002 and has served on the American Bar Association Commission on Minorities in the Profession, Standing Committee on Public Education, and Standing Committee on the Federal Judiciary. His community service includes his recent term as chair of the Board of Trustees of Greater Baltimore Healthcare Inc. from 2011 to 2014. He is resident in the firm's Baltimore office.*

Acknowledgment: *I would like to thank partners Gardner Duvall, Warren Weaver, and Tiffany Releford, recruitment coordinator Susan Bolyard, and intern Shannon Werbek for their contributions to this chapter.*

Elements of a Robust Strategic Diversity Plan: Leadership, a Roadmap, and Buy-In

Asker A. Saeed

Director, Diversity

Day Pitney LLP

ASPATORE

Introduction

Large law firms can no longer rely on the hard work and good intentions of a self-selected few to create an environment where diversity is valued and inclusion is a cornerstone for future success. Like with any other successful initiative taken on by an institution, there must be a strategic plan created by someone with expertise, adopted by the leadership of the institution, and implemented by everyone. Furthermore, the strategic plan must function as a deliberate effort to upset the historical approach which, by all accounts, has not yielded desired results.

This chapter will discuss important elements of a strategic diversity plan, including: having someone in charge with the ability to allocate resources consistently with the plan; having a plan that is consistent with the firm's position in the legal market and overall operational goals; and gaining buy-in not just from leaders at the firm but from everyone who can play a role.

Having Someone in Charge

If a law firm could only do one thing to improve their diversity initiative, it would be this: hire someone to be in charge and hold them accountable by paying them to lead the effort and achieve results. Although this approach is becoming more common (particularly in large national law firms), many firms are still choosing to operate under the old model of designating a partner with a particular interest in the issues (identified either by expression or minority status) and asking that person to drive the firm's efforts. Some firms are experiencing success with this model, but logic would dictate that law firms would be able to achieve far more success if they had someone with a deep understanding of the issues and challenges of the law firm environment leading and devoting all of their time to the effort. There are three key elements to the position:

1. the title must make clear the role is a senior position at the firm and is at the same level as other senior leaders (e.g., in business development, information services, and/or professional development), and the title must be consistent with the firm's commitment to the effort and willingness to allocate resources to the effort;

2. the role must come with a dedicated budget controlled by the diversity leader; and

3. the person hired must have a demonstrated and proven track record in working towards greater diversity and inclusion at an institution, in the legal profession generally, or at another services-oriented profession.

Proper titling is essential, as it serves as a statement both internally and externally as to the firm's commitment to the effort. Bringing in a "diversity manager" to join a group of "directors" and "officers" suggests the diversity effort is not as highly regarded by the firm as other initiatives. Conversely, bringing in a "director of diversity" or a "chief diversity officer" while at the same time not giving that person the institutional respect that would come with such a position will only serve to demoralize and ultimately undermine the effort and its legitimacy. A dedicated budget, controlled by the diversity leader, ensures resources will only be spent in a manner consistent with the plan and, more importantly, that the firm's diversity efforts are not controlled by any one person's personal involvement with an organization or cause, but rather by the firm as an institution's involvement with an organization or cause. And since dedicated diversity leaders in law firms is a relatively new phenomenon, there are very few people in the market with actual law firm diversity experience. That said, firms should be very careful to only hire someone to take on this role who has experience dealing with the issues (and not solely because they are diverse themselves). This is particularly important when hiring a woman, person of color, or member of the LGBT community, as their diverse status could easily be interpreted as the only qualification necessary (thereby undermining the entire initiative and likelihood of success). Without these three key elements in place, the diversity leader will not have the respect nor the tools to succeed in the position and advance the effort.

Have a Plan Focusing on Systems, Procedures, and Operational Customs as the Primary Vehicle for Achieving Desired Results

The traditional approach in large law firms has been to "win hearts and minds" in an effort to rally well-intentioned people to "do the right thing" in furtherance of diversity and inclusion. But this approach has yielded limited results. Over the last fifteen years, there have been hundreds of panels, seminars, and general discussions on how to succeed at diversifying large law firms and, although the focus of the discussion is typically around general lack of commitment to the cause, perhaps the real culprit is this: the way law firms do business, not with clients but with their employees' career development, is just not conducive to diversity.

Law firms have essentially been operating the same way for decades. Certainly technology has made the practice much more efficient and client demands have added a new twist on the economics, but the model of lawyers billing clients for time spent on legal matters all while operating on the direction of a large group of partners who double as managers and leaders has remained more or less unchanged for a very long time. So essentially the law firm business model of today is not a whole lot different from the law firm business model of yesteryear. And since the business model we use today was developed at a time when there was virtually no diversity in the legal profession (at least not on the gender, race, sexual orientation, or disability front), is it any wonder that diversity and particularly inclusion at large law firms has remain unchanged for decades? It is not enough to just *want* to change, firms must start doing things differently to achieve diversity and inclusion goals. Any firm looking at operational functions to tweak need look no further than the billable hour (which I would posit is the number-one factor working against diversity at large law firms).

To be sure, there is nothing intrinsically wrong with billing clients for time spent on their legal matters, and it may indeed be the best way to generate revenue for the firm. However, when the billable hour is used as the primary tool for evaluating one's value provided to the organization, it serves to perpetuate the diversity problem. Every time an associate (and invariably, a diverse associate) is told "You need to balance your time better" or "You should do all that diversity stuff but it will not count toward your billable hours (and therefore will not count towards your bonus and career progression)" or "You should be doing it to advance your career and not for recognition here at the firm," the actual message being sent is that the firm does not value those efforts, or at least will not value that time the same as time actually billed to the client. Again, that position is clearly justifiable on an economic basis, but the impact of that position on the firm's diversity efforts and ability to retain diverse lawyers is profound and amplified since (a) almost by definition "diverse" lawyers are more likely to have diverse interests in addition to professional interests they will want to pursue to feel professionally fulfilled, and (b) the firm's clients, government organizations, and other legal entities are actively looking to diversify their own ranks by poaching diverse associates at large law firms with the promise of valuing more than just the amount of time spent billing clients. Furthermore, in a law firm setting, who gets the work is largely at the discretion of the partner who generates the work. Although the associate's experiences and expertise play a large part, often unconscious biases steer that work towards a certain demographic. And when law firm associates rely almost exclusively on someone else (i.e., partners) to supply them with the one element that impacts their career progression the most (i.e., billable work), the potential for institutional and unconscious biases to wreak havoc on a women's or lawyer of color's career progression is dramatic.

Defining one's value based on how many hours he or she works, coupled with most law firms' lack of a pyramid management structure, can cause real problems for a diversity and inclusion initiative. Unlike in a company where there is a president and a team of direct reports who run the company, law firms are typically run by a small governing body that decides which of them is going to be out in front (and be designated as the managing partner or chairman of the firm). On the surface, these two models seem similar, but in the company everyone who works at the company ultimately works for the president, whereas in a law firm, although the staff and non-partner attorneys clearly work for someone, it is unclear who they actually work for. In the case of staff, is it their supervisor? Or the attorneys they support? In the case of non-partners, which of the many partners they do work for do they actually work for? And who do the partners work for? Clearly not the small governing body or the managing partner or the chair of the firm. As a result, since there is no clearly defined organizational chart, changes to the way the firm does business through a new policy or procedure is not only met with skepticism (since "that is not the way we do things"), but also the unfortunate reality that it may or may not be adhered to and with, at least for some people, no expectation of negative consequences as a result.

In fairness, attempting to completely overhaul the law firm business model is not the answer. That is just not a realistic goal. However, law firms would be well served to pay less attention to "rallying the troops" and more attention to their systems, procedures, and operational customs with an eye toward analyzing as to effectiveness when applied to women, people of color, members of the LGBT community, and people with disabilities.

Focusing on a law firm's systems, procedures, and operational customs is an essential component to executing a strategic diversity plan. A good strategic diversity plan should be tailored to the particular firm, taking into account situational factors such as size, geographic location, and type of practice. Below are four components to a strategic diversity plan that should be considered:

Branding

Law firms are for-profit entities. The goal is to maximize shareholder revenues. Any effort taken on by the firm must ultimately provide the necessary shareholder return. The best way for a law firm's diversity initiative to provide shareholder return is to make sure clients, and particularly the ones with a stated commitment to diversity and inclusion and to only working with vendors with a similar commitment, potential recruits, diverse and otherwise, and media, fully understand the initiative's goals and successes. Firms need to distinguish themselves from competitors by establishing themselves in their markets as the firm most committed to the diversity and inclusion initiative. Examples of easy things a firm can do are: establishing employee resource groups, offering benefits to support a diverse population, holding internal events designed to celebrate the diversity of the firm and/or communities in which the firm operates, and getting involved in the business community's diversity efforts. Harder things might include creating programs designed to improve the likelihood of attorneys of color achieving partnership, hiring someone to run the initiative and devoting significant financial resources to the success of the initiative, and monetarily rewarding people who get involved in the initiative.

Recruiting

There is no question that recruiting attorneys of color, either at entry level or laterally, is a key component of any diversity strategy. But ultimately the best recruiting approach is to focus on recruiting lawyers and staff who will support the diversity initiative regardless of whether they are diverse. The goal is not just to have diverse people working at the firm, but to create an environment where people who care about diversity will want to work and succeed. Furthermore, placing emphasis on bringing in diverse people has the potential to encourage bad behavior (i.e., bringing in diverse people because they are diverse and then not giving them the support needed to succeed). Firms should also consider implementing a policy to ensure all lateral hiring is done from adequately diverse slates with the emphasis on interviewing diverse slates and hiring the best candidate for the position.

Supporting

Law firms are constantly being asked by affinity bar associations, law student organizations, and other community organizations to sponsor banquets, award ceremonies, seminars, and other similar events. These sponsorships are not only vital to the success of these mostly volunteer organizations (many of which are led by lawyers from large law firms), but they also serve as an important vehicle for demonstrating a firm's commitment to the effort and success of the organization. That said, firms should sponsor organizations strategically and not on a case-by-case basis based on whether a partner or other lawyer is involved in the organization or a particular client is supportive of a particular organization. Giving some thought at the outset as to where the dollars will be spent (for example, a regional firm might decide to only support the local chapters of the minority bar associations in the areas where the firm practices rather than support the national organization, or a national firm may choose to only support the national organization and the local chapters in the areas where the firm has a major presence) and on which organizations (for example, minority lawyer organizations in the region or state where the firm practices and law student organizations at law schools the firm recruits from regardless of whether the firm has a presence in that area, and not community-based organizations) will go a long way to the cohesiveness of the spend, which in turn will greatly increase the likelihood of shareholder return.

Clients

Law firms exist to serve clients. Obviously this is done primarily through legal services. But in this day and age when in-house legal departments are just as focused on their diversity initiative (particularly as it operates within the greater company's diversity initiative), it would behoove a large law firm to look for opportunities to support its client's efforts. And that means going beyond simply answering requests for demographic information. Easy things a law firm can do include inviting clients to join the firm as a guest at the many events the firm sponsors, recommending a client for a speaking opportunity, and asking clients to participate in the law firm's initiatives. Harder things might include offering resources and expertise to their clients, co-hosting panels and seminars, and including the diversity leader in interactions with clients (particularly on pitches and beauty pageants).

A strategic diversity plan containing well thought out components that are appropriate for the firm's situational characteristics and that focuses on the firm's systems, procedures, and operational customs will not only provide a roadmap for success, but it will also go a long way to securing broad institutional buy-in.

Securing Buy-In Not Just from Firm Leaders, but from the Entire Institution

Focusing on systems, procedures, and operational customs helps institutionalize the effort to become more diverse and inclusive. Having someone in charge capably leading the effort with the support of firm leadership is essential. But in an environment that looks more like a large group of independent contractors with shared overhead, clients, and basic values, the more people willing to support the effort, the more likelihood the effort will succeed.

Historically, diversity efforts at large law firms have centered on the notion that there is something wrong with a white male-dominated system that favors the success of white men and that the institution must figure out how to spread the opportunity around so women and people of color are able to achieve their fair share of that success. Although that is true, the more effective sentiment would be that we are all in this together and that more women and people of color succeeding at the firm is not only good for women and people of color but for all of us (including white males). That shifts the perspective from taking something away from one group to give to another group, to creating more opportunities for everyone. To that end, it is very important that, in addition to creating initiatives designed to advance the careers of diverse lawyers, a firm institute changes to or new policies, systems, and operational customs designed to benefit the entire attorney population as well. For example, a firm could implement a sponsorship program for attorneys of color and a work distribution program designed to ensure good quality work for all lawyers (including lawyers of color). Ultimately, diversity is not a minority thing; it is an everybody thing. Programs designed to improve everyone's experience necessarily also improve diverse lawyers' experiences. And since we all stand to benefit, we all have a role to play.

Most people at a large law firm will fall into one of four categories when considering their involvement in the diversity and inclusion initiative: leader, supporter, bystander, or obstructer. A diversity leader should spend most of his or her time working with bystanders. The leaders have been leading since before the firm's diversity leader got there and will likely continue to do so (with or without support from the diversity leader). The supporters support the leaders (for a variety of reasons, including some unrelated to the diversity initiative) and will continue to do so somewhat regardless of an institutional position. The obstructers are so few in number and likely of a demographic that would suggest they will not be around for very long anyway. The bystanders are not only likely the largest group but also the group most dominated by white men (and, not coincidentally, power brokers). This is a group made up mostly of well-intentioned white men who either do not think they can play a role in a diversity and inclusion initiative or, if they do, just do not have any idea how to get on the bandwagon. Converting bystanders into supporters and even leaders is an effective way to turn the tide at a law firm and get the ball rolling towards an institutionalization of the effort. This is best accomplished through communication, either firm-wide or one-on-one. But before engaging through communication, the diversity leader must create a "safe space" for people at all levels to discuss their concerns without fear of ridicule or consequence.

Conclusion

Large law firms have suffered from lack of diversity and inclusion for a long time. If a firm is willing to admit it has a problem, recognize that its internal systems, policies, and operational customs are in large part to blame, and do the hard work required to level the playing field, creating an environment where diversity matters and inclusion is a reality is a very achievable paradigm.

Key Takeaways

- Hire someone with expertise to serve as your diversity leader (instead of relying on someone in the firm who gets paid to bill clients and bring in revenue), and equip that person with the resources and clout to advance the effort.

- Focus on improving your policies, systems, and operational customs so that, at the very least, they do not discriminate against diverse lawyers and ideally they work to advance the careers of your diverse lawyers while at the same time the careers of your non-diverse lawyers as well.

- Have a strategy for how the firm's resources (both monetary and otherwise) will be used, and stick to it.

- Emphasize that diversity is not a minority thing; it is an everybody thing. Everyone stands to benefit from creating a culture where diversity and inclusion matter and are valued, and everyone can play a role in advancing the effort.

Asker A. Saeed is the director of diversity at Day Pitney LLP, a northeast regional law firm with nine offices in Connecticut, New Jersey, Boston, New York City, and Washington, DC. As a member of the firm's senior management team, he is responsible for developing and implementing the firm's strategic diversity plan and serving as a key thought leader, ambassador, and advocate on diversity, inclusion, and equity, all while keeping diversity at the forefront of all of the firm's initiatives. Additionally, he leads the firm's efforts to identify, develop, and foster relationships among various external constituencies who are active in diversity and inclusion, including firm clients, bar associations, and affinity groups. He also actively supports and collaborates with the firm's Women Working Together, Day Pitney Attorneys of Color, and Day Pitney Alliance initiatives.

Mr. Saeed joined Day Pitney from United Technologies Corporation's Pratt & Whitney division, where he was most recently vice president of customer business, commercial at IAE International Aero Engines AG, a Pratt & Whitney joint venture. Prior to that, he was lead counsel for the global leasing and finance organizations at IAE and managed all corporate governance matters for the joint venture. Prior to joining IAE, he was assistant counsel in the Commercial Engines and Global Services Section of Pratt & Whitney. While at Pratt & Whitney, he coordinated all legal department diversity efforts and was designated by the general counsel as the legal department's representative to the UTC Diversity Council. Mr. Saeed began his legal career as an associate at two large northeast regional law firms based in Hartford, Connecticut, where he was an active member of the diversity and recruiting committees.

Mr. Saeed is a founding member and past president of the South Asian Bar Association of Connecticut and served on the executive committee of the South Asian Bar Association of North America. Currently he is an advisory committee member of the Connecticut Hispanic Bar Association, a board member of the Tri-State Diversity Council, and a member of the Association of Law Firm Diversity Professionals. In addition, he has been a frequent speaker on diversity and career development issues, both locally and nationally, and has presented on topics such as "Diversity Best Practices," "Charting Your Own Course," "Succeeding within Firm and Corporate Cultures," "The Work/Life Balance," and "How to Advance and Make an Impact as an In-House Lawyer."

Micro-Inequities, Intersectionality, Covering, Diversity, and Talent Management: Lessons from One Diverse Attorney's Experience

Michelle Wimes

Director, Professional Development and Inclusion
Ogletree Deakins Nash Smoak & Stewart PC

ASPATORE

Introduction

Law firms believe they have moved past a debate concerning the value of diversity and are now focused on creating and sustaining inclusive work environments. But these inclusive work environments do not happen organically, and they will remain elusive as long as a firm's diversity efforts are siloed from the firm's other strategic imperatives and as long as diverse lawyers continue to have hushed conversations among themselves about the challenges they face. This chapter explores what can happen when diverse lawyers become their authentic selves, share their stories of difference, and advocate for more inclusion. It also highlights what happens when law firms approach diversity and inclusion strategically with a willingness to hear and learn from those stories.

My twenty-year journey has helped me uncover many lessons about workplace environments, leadership, career ownership, resilience, diversity, and professional development. In this chapter, I offer reflections on the following:

- *Micro-inequities:* The forces of micro-inequities, those cumulative repeated behaviors that devalue, discourage, and impair workplace performance, are real but are not destabilizing if properly addressed.
- *Authenticity:* Resisting the urge to cover and seizing the benefits of authenticity can pay enormous career dividends for the diverse performer.
- *Relationships:* Building strong workplace relationships is vital for decoding and navigating the social and professional structure of today's law firm.
- *Affinity groups:* Law firm affinity groups can be impactful if they have the courage to candidly confront the unmet needs of their constituents.
- *Mentoring:* Mentoring can thrive in law firms, provided we provide time-constrained partners tools to enable their mentorship.
- *Diversity and professional development:* Efforts directed to diversity and professional development are best viewed as sources of competitive advantage for today's law firm, undertaken with the same level of strategic focus witnessed in its commercial objectives.

There are stories of difference, covering, and micro-inequities that never get told or talked about publicly. Minority lawyers, including women, sometimes feel safe enough to share these experiences among ourselves, but hardly ever feel emboldened or impassioned enough to share them with the majority. Why? Because we fear that our stories will be marginalized or that we will be seen as being too sensitive, complainers, or better yet, victims of our own histories.

I know too many seasoned lawyers who still carry the burden of being treated differently, and have attempted to bury their pain, hurt, and disillusionment by keeping silent and simply doing whatever they can to blend into the majority, to assimilate. Therein lies the problem. Unless we as minorities and women start to tell our stories in our own voices and learn how to leverage our differences, a fundamental understanding and support for diversity programs, policies, and initiatives will remain elusive.

Somehow we have all colluded to make stories of differential treatment unspeakable, and by doing so we have given them more power. Their survival feeds off not talking about them. By sharing our stories, we make them a necessary part of the conversation. It is time to peel back the layers of pain and discuss the real stories behind the facade.

There is so much power in storytelling. Because as radical as it may be perceived, stories help us understand the realities people face and endure in their personal and professional lives. They can help us delve more deeply into the mindset needed to overcome would-be barriers and, in the process, understand why diversity and inclusion efforts are important, why these efforts seem to have stalled, and what might be done to reinvigorate them to ensure they meet the needs of those for whom they are targeted.

Embracing Authenticity: We Are Defined by the Challenges We Overcome

I graduated from law school over twenty years ago. In my fourteen years of work as a practicing attorney, first as an associate and then of counsel and later as an equity partner, there have been myriad challenges. One of the biggest challenges for me professionally has been the double whammy of being a racial minority as well as a woman in a field that is predominated by white men.

Twenty years ago, I was reading and dissecting Kimberlé Crenshaw's work on intersectionality because, as an African-American woman, I felt left out of the discourse. The focus then seemed to be on the impact of women entering the profession in larger numbers than ever before. Then the focus evolved to a discussion about the lack of racial and ethnic minorities, especially in the upper echelons of Am Law 100 firms and Fortune 100 companies. Hardly ever was there a discussion about the specific challenges faced by women of color or other double (or even triple) minorities.

Intersectionality has been defined as "the interplay of race, class, and gender, often resulting in multiple dimensions of disadvantage." Crenshaw's work in the area of critical race theory was the missing lens I needed. I felt my unique experience as an African-American woman was validated. Later, after leaving the practice of law to become a diversity professional, I felt much the same way after reading the groundbreaking research and work of Dr. Arin Reeves and the American Bar Association on women of color in the legal profession. Dr. Arin Reeves et al., "Visible Invisibility: Women of Color in Law Firms" (2006); the American Bar Association, "From Visible Invisibility to Visibly Successful" (2008).

My first experience with these intersecting identities came very early in my professional career. After having completed the first semester of law school, I interviewed for a summer associate position with a toney Midwestern law firm and began that clerkship the summer after my first year of law school. One of the most exciting things about being a summer associate at a law firm was being treated like a true lawyer in terms of office size and salary. So, as superficial as it sounds, I was looking forward to this. I grew up with both parents, neither of whom had a college degree, but both of whom had very stable government jobs. I knew no one in my immediate family or circle who had his or her own office, was a lawyer, or made anything close to the salaries lawyers made in law firm practice.

On the first day of work, after orientation, each one of us was taken around to our individual offices. As we stopped by each office to drop off each summer intern, we all "ooohd" and "aaahd" at the offices each of us were to inhabit. They were nice and quite spacious. I was the last person to be shown my office and, unlike my cohorts, all of whom were white and two of whom were also female, I was given a much smaller and less elegant paralegal's office with no fanfare or explanation.

It was a devastating blow to an inexperienced intern who expected that the playing field would be level from the get-go. Though dismayed, I set up my office and went to work. I did not know if I had been given a smaller office because I was the only black, the only black female, or the only first-year law student. I assumed the latter and worked even harder that summer to demonstrate both to myself and to the lawyers at the firm that they did not make a mistake in hiring me. My work was stellar and at the end of the summer I was offered a position for the summer following my second year of law school.

Why, after twenty-plus years of having been out of law school, should this even matter to me? Why do I remember this situation so well all these years later? Because it was the first time in my professional career that I remember not feeling good enough. It was a subtle, devaluing message, a micro-inequity, that did not need to be communicated verbally, but there it was in full view for everyone to see. Every time one of my fellow interns walked past my office or came in to chat with me, what must my physical surroundings have communicated to them? What about the attorneys for whom I worked? I was dogged all summer, if only in my head, by the questions of whether I was good enough to be there, whether I deserved the job, whether I had what it took to be successful, whether I was an "affirmative action" hire, whether they just needed me to pad their numbers. After all, I met two criterion: I was black and I was a woman.

It would have been easy for me to sit in my office drowning in my "first world" problem, feeling sorry for myself. It would have been easy to isolate myself from my co-workers, just keep my head down and try to "do good work." I toyed with complaining to someone, but then I worried about reinforcing the stereotype of the "angry black woman," so I decided to stay quiet. Yet, all these questions circling in my mind, all these unspoken questions that it seemed I, alone, had to deal with, were the background noise in my head. Things I had to willfully ignore and overcome just to do my work.

I told myself I belonged. But, in truth, I felt like a fraud, and now that I look back on it, I was covering. I did not want to stand out any more than I already did. I was the only black, the only black female, the only first-year law student, and the only student from a national law school.

Kenji Yoshino defines covering as toning down a disfavored identity to fit into the mainstream. That summer, I toned down my "blackness" as much as I could. I never told anyone I grew up on the east side of town. I never told anyone my parents were not professionals. I code-switched all day, every day. I had a different tone, demeanor, and language during the day as opposed to when I arrived at my parents' home weary after a long day of being my inauthentic self. I lived in two worlds. The posh, toney world where I was making a lawyer's salary, the equivalent of $4,000 a month, and the world where I would often awaken to the sounds of police sirens and gunfire in the wee hours of the morning.

Cultivating a Mindset of Persistence and Positivity While Building Strong Relationships

In spite of my environment, one thing my parents cultivated in me was a mindset of positivity and persistence. You simply did not quit even when it seemed you were in over your head, and furthermore, a victim mentality simply was not an option in our household. So, that summer, in spite of how I felt inside, I chose to be engaged. I went on the summer associate float trip, a first for me. I cheered my colleagues on as they played in the summer baseball league (I abhor baseball, which is why I did not play). I wined and dined with clients, law firm partners, and my peers. I worked hard, was given plum assignments, much-needed critical feedback, and at the end of the summer, I earned an offer to return the summer after my second year of law school. And that second summer resulted in another earned offer for permanent employment upon graduation.

As I recall, another professional experience with my intersecting identities that still stands out for me happened during the first few weeks as a new associate. After passing the bar exam, I began my career with eight other newly minted lawyers. Because our office building was undergoing renovations at the time, we were all forced to share three conference room spaces as temporary offices for a few months. Thus, there were three attorneys in each conference room, each with their own desks, telephones, and chairs. I shared my space with two white male peers.

From the first day of permanent employment, I saw a difference in the demeanor of some of the firm's white male lawyers toward me as opposed to my two colleagues. Everyone was friendly to me, of course. I knew many of them from my summer associate experiences. Here is what I noticed though. My two white male colleagues were consistently asked to lunch on an almost daily basis. More importantly, they were offered to tag along at depositions, court appearances, and client meetings. Not once did anyone, either my peers or the partners, think to invite me. I do not think it was intentional, and I certainly did not jump to the conclusion that it was because of my race or sex. I assumed it probably had to do with the fact that they had been hired to work in one practice group (litigation), whereas I had been hired to work in another (immigration/labor and employment).

But the voices in my head that I had attempted to quiet returned. They challenged me: "Why is this happening? Is it only happening to me? How do I find out? Am I being too sensitive? Am I overreacting? Am I a fraud? Do I really deserve to be here?" I had so many conversations with myself during those first few weeks of employment.

I handled that situation as I had been trained, by maintaining a positive attitude and taking charge of the situation. I reached out to two partners with whom I had developed relationships during my prior two summer internships with the firm and I asked for the same experiences and exposure. What I learned from that experience was that as a young lawyer, in spite of your insecurities and self-doubt, you cannot be afraid to step out and ask for what you want because many times, if you do not, you will miss the opportunity to develop professionally. You must take ownership of your career and affirmatively seek the experiences and opportunities that will allow you to grow and develop. And you must align yourself with mentors to get the information you need and sponsors who can advocate successfully on your behalf.

I experienced firsthand that shared affinity breeds familiarity and comfort, which most often directly correlates to a broader range of professional development opportunities for those with the shared affinity. That realization caused me to take it upon myself to get to know others better. I strove to find opportunities for shared experiences that would help deepen my connections and relationships within the firm. Had I not shared office space with my white male colleagues, I wonder how long it would have taken me to realize I was not getting the same kind of informal learning opportunities. To this day, I shudder to think about the potential cumulative impact on my career.

Reflecting back on these two discrete experiences, the law firm could have done a number of things better. First, the law firm should have assigned me a mentor, both during my summer associate and first-year associate experiences. A mentor could have acted as a sounding board to help quell some of the questions and doubts that were circling in my head and taking up too much space and time. Frankly, this is space and time that could have and should have been dedicated to honing my legal skills. Second, the law firm should have had a better onboarding process. Ideally, this process would have not only identified early experiences that all newly (but especially diverse) lawyers would need to give them a firm foundation, but would have ensured that the opportunities were dispersed more evenly.

Leveraging Differences, Overcoming Micro-Inequities, and Building Confidence

The bigger lesson I took away from my intersecting identities was to learn that I could capitalize and leverage my difference within the broader legal community. I did not have to allow the law firm to define me as a person or determine my value. During the first few years of my practice with the firm, I became active in the local civic and bar community. I helped start a nationally recognized charter school and became board vice president, which fostered my leadership skills. I volunteered to take on pro bono cases through the Volunteer Attorney Project, which helped hone my writing, communication, and advocacy skills. I helped the local African-American bar association establish their inaugural scholarship program for minority law students, which nurtured a budding interest in legal diversity issues. I helped run student mediation programs in local high schools, which improved my negotiation skills. I staffed "Ask a Lawyer Telethons" providing free community legal advice, which refined my critical thinking and analytical skills. In short order, I began to build a reputation for getting things done outside the law firm which, in turn, increased my confidence and helped bolster my performance within the law firm.

Law firms should encourage all lawyers to build their skills, connections, and relationships both inside and outside the law firm. This is especially important for diverse lawyers who are not likely to inherit books of business from senior lawyers in the firm. In addition to focusing on becoming great lawyers with a firm understanding of the substantive law, diverse lawyers should be encouraged to nurture their networks early and often.

Moreover, law firms should not expect diverse lawyers to look like, sound like, or act like majority lawyers. Diverse lawyers bring different perspectives, backgrounds, and experiences to the table. Law firms need to recognize that diversity will look and sound differently, and thus firms need to give diverse lawyers room to feel confident enough to share those experiences and leverage them to the good of the firm and the firm's clients. Why hire a diverse lawyer in the first place if you just expect them to assimilate and be like every other lawyer in your firm? *See* Verna Myers, "What If I Say the Wrong Thing: 25 Habits for Culturally Effective People" (2014).

In spite of my increased confidence gained from my extracurricular legal activities, the intersecting identities of my gender and age provided fodder for other micro-inequities. Being a young, aggressive woman litigator in a profession dominated by older men was not easy. Many times I arrived in court only to be shown to the court reporter's station or asked if I was the paralegal accompanying the attorney, who obviously had not yet arrived. While six months pregnant with my first child and trying a sexual harassment case for my client, the judge, an older white male, addressed me in open court as "Little Missy." Because I was often underestimated, I compensated with over-preparation. I was extremely knowledgeable about the case law and my client's desires. I knew I had to be twice as good as any white male or female lawyer who opposed me.

I also found that there was not necessarily a natural bond while working for and with senior female lawyers. Our shared gender should have been a commonality that created greater solidarity, but this was not always the case. Sometimes I felt that my weaknesses were purposefully highlighted by senior women for whom I worked. At other times, I felt something akin to disdain, as if these women believed I did not have to work as hard as they had to work to achieve the very same thing. There was only one African-American female partner in the entire firm at the time. And, unfortunately, she did not want to have anything to do with me. She did not go out of her way to get to know me, she did not attend any firm functions, and when I managed to secure some free time on her calendar to meet with her, she was curt. I was hurt. She would not be the mentor or sponsor I longed for.

Creating Meaningful and Impactful Affinity Groups

Many firms now have strong women's initiatives that are designed to mentor younger women lawyers and be a resource to them as they navigate internal firm politics and learn to be business developers, the key to career progression. I believe that women's initiatives do a disservice to young women lawyers if they do not talk candidly about the challenges women face in a predominantly male environment and equip them to deal with those challenges. Sharing past experiences and positive stories of triumph can be very uplifting and inspiring to younger lawyers. Senior female lawyers should not make it to the top and lift up the ladder when they get there. And law firms do a disservice to young minority lawyers when they bring them into environments where there is little to no representation of them in the senior leadership ranks. It is hard to be what you cannot see.

During my first year of practice, I found myself working primarily for one senior woman in an area of law, immigration, that required much attention to detail, an ungodly amount of paperwork, and very little client contact. Moreover, the partner was so busy that she had very little time to train me. I had participated in an immigration law clinic in law school, but the emphasis was on family law immigration and political asylum cases, not business law immigration.

To be fair, I did not do enough research on my own to know the differences between the various types of immigration law or to understand how the law firm's immigration practice varied from my law school training. I was simply excited to have found a firm in the Midwest that did this kind of work. Moreover, I believed I would be able to use my Spanish-speaking skills (I had majored in Spanish in college), but all of our clients were

French nationals who were either engineers or scientists and needed non-immigrant business visas.

In short, I was not prepared for how mundane the work would be. I was not happy, and my work showed it. I sometimes made sloppy, avoidable mistakes. She obviously had a right not to fully trust my work. But her demeanor and tone toward me made the situation worse. She was condescending more than encouraging, flippant more than informative, dismissive and sometimes just downright mean. Of course, I started to doubt and second-guess myself. I was terrified that I would be crucified during my evaluation, and I realized there would be no one else to acknowledge the things I had done well. My stomach was in knots almost every day; I questioned my decision to become a lawyer. I thought about quitting the practice of law regularly. And I was afraid to talk to others about my experiences. There was no diversity professional or talent manager with whom I could confide. There was no senior diverse female lawyer with whom I could commiserate either. I felt wholly alone.

Seeking Critical Feedback to Develop Requisite Skills

Here is what I learned from that experience. As a diverse associate, you should never give one partner that much power over your career. Work for as many partners as you can, gain as much experience as you can so your work can be judged holistically from multiple angles by multiple partners. Also, working with a broader group of people enables one to build solid relationships across a wide spectrum. These relationships will prove invaluable for continued mentoring and ultimately the sponsorship necessary to earn one's place into the hallowed halls of partnership.

From the law firm perspective, at least in the first couple of years of a diverse attorney's practice, it is helpful to have someone in charge who is looking at who that attorney is working with, what kinds of experiences he or she is getting, and having periodic check-ins. This ensures that the lawyer is getting good work assignments and the critical feedback necessary to develop his or her substantive expertise. Moreover, it allows the firm to catch and correct situations like mine before they de-escalate out of control.

Fortunately, I did not permit this experience to deflate me or extinguish my desire for success. The bottom line was I had simply worked too hard to get where I was, and I was not going to let one person, a few mistakes, and/or my own insecurities derail my career. And my persistence and refusal to be a victim of my own circumstance paid off. After surmising the situation, I got to work. I switched practice groups.

Because I had been a teacher for two years prior to law school, I found a natural fit with the firm's Education and School Law Practice Group. I blossomed and excelled. There were no formal talent management or professional development programs to learn how to take depositions, conduct fact witness interviews, write position statements, respond to discovery requests, or write summary judgment motions or briefs. It was all trial by fire. I learned by watching the partners and then jumping in and just doing it. And I absolutely loved it. I successfully second-chaired jury trials, and I first- and second-chaired a number of teacher termination hearings. I won all sorts of dispositive motions for my clients, and my fact witness investigations led to powerful position statements and even better depositions.

In short, I became the "go-to" young lawyer on my team. I had myriad client opportunities; I helped recruit and mentor new lawyers. I felt like an important and vital part of the team and firm. My evaluations were stellar; I became a top performer. I enjoyed my work because I found it meaningful. I also enjoyed it because I was mentored and sponsored by two senior male partners, one white and one black, who fully trusted me and challenged me. Because I knew they believed in me and wanted the best for me, I sought critical feedback regularly, even when they were busy. As a result, I always knew where I stood and what I needed to do to improve. I simply flourished.

Providing Time-Constrained Partners with Effective Mentoring Tools

There are a few lessons I learned from this experience. One, which should seem obvious today but is not, is that neither mentors nor sponsors have to be the same sex or race as the mentee or protégée. A mentor is simply someone who is willing to share vital information and resources to help you become a better lawyer. A sponsor is willing to put their credibility on the line to support your advancement.

Second, partners should tell lawyers, both diverse and majority, when they are top performers. Firms should identify and invest in those top performers. Provide them with opportunities to deepen their skill sets. Too often, a law firm's professional development opportunities tend to focus on those lawyers who are underperforming or on life support. This drains a firm's resources and, quite frankly, can undermine the firm's diversity efforts.

Perhaps the biggest lesson I learned from my own experience is that law firm partners need to give ongoing critical feedback to diverse lawyers to help them develop and grow. Partners cannot be afraid they will run afoul of discrimination laws if they are candid with diverse lawyers. They do a disservice to the diverse lawyer and the firm if they do not hold diverse associates to the same standards as majority associates. Moreover, partners cannot assume that critical feedback will scare diverse associates away. When a bond of trust between partner and diverse associate has been established, these associates welcome and crave the feedback.

Werten Bellamy, president of Stakeholders Inc., a premier legal consulting firm, has developed the concept of "feed forward." Feed forward "involves developing the practice of actively seeking advice for the future." In essence, Werten urges associates to take ownership of their careers and empower themselves by curating the information needed from partners to successfully "confront new challenges, build new skills, and cultivate new relationships." (Werten Bellamy, "Mentoring Moments: A Matter of Building Windmills," PD Quarterly, November 2014.)

How is this done? By recognizing that partner time to mentor is limited, and associates are encouraged to target a specific developmental need, and then proactively seek the partner's advice via a fifteen- to twenty-minute "mentoring moment" to learn how that partner confronted a similar obstacle, built the same skill, or relationship. This novel concept acknowledges that associates need more than the sporadic informal "feedback" and/or annual formal evaluation to succeed, especially when there are ever-increasing constraints on partners' time and resources because of a law firm's laser focus on productivity and profitability and the client's focus on cost-effectiveness. I know now that my actions in seeking critical advice from my two mentors was nothing more than me employing Werten's "feed forward" concept. And my career took off because of it.

I gave birth to my first two daughters during my third and fifth year of practice and automatically inherited another intersecting identity, that of working mother. During my first pregnancy, I was asked more than once by my male peers whether I intended to return to work full-time after the birth of my child. Frankly, I was shocked by this question the first time I heard it. The working women in my life experiences, admittedly all African-American, had all returned to work after birthing their babies. Why would I be any different? It never crossed my mind that I would not return to work full-time, so that is exactly what I did after the birth of both babies. Of course, representing public and private school districts made my practice a little more predictable. Much of my work consisted of advice and counseling, internal investigations, and motion writing. And there was some downtime in the summer when school was out, as well as over the holiday breaks.

But all of that changed once I became a mom three times over. By that time, I had been recruited away to work for an AmLaw 100 firm as a senior associate. I began doing expert witness development work on product liability cases filed against our clients in Latin American courts. My Spanish-speaking skills, coupled with a prosecutor husband who had a much more predictable schedule, made this my dream job. I often found myself in some exotic location (think Rio, Brazil or San Jose, Costa Rica) pinching my own arm at my incredible good fortune. Not one person asked me how I would travel abroad regularly with two babies under the age of two. I just did it. And, in the process, I had complete professional discretion and autonomy. I was deeply trusted by my peers and partners with whom I worked. I continued working full-time, traveling abroad regularly, and ultimately helping our clients win their cases.

Sponsoring Diverse Lawyers: A Win-Win Situation

When our international work wound down, I transitioned to an of counsel position in the firm's labor and employment practice group and gave birth to my third daughter. That was the first and only time I ever worried about not being able to meet my billable hour requirement. In my mind, two children were manageable, but I feared I would lose balance with three. Soon after returning from maternity leave, I was recruited by a smaller regional firm to help develop their education law practice. I decided to join the firm as a reduced hours partner. This decision was an easy one for me given that my current firm did not have a way at the time to make partner on a reduced hours schedule.

I was one of two African-American partners in the entire firm and the only reduced hours partner. I helped start the firm's first diversity committee and was an active member of the Women in Business affinity group. I spent nearly five years there focusing on special education matters for my clients. Frankly, were it not for the sponsorship of a senior white female partner (with whom I had worked as an associate at my prior firm) who used her own political clout and book of business to bring me in as a partner (even though I had no business of my own, only subject matter expertise and relationships with her existing clients), I would not have hit the ground running. She sponsored me by slicing off a portion of her business, giving me origination, managing, and working credit, and the opportunity to build the business. In that first year alone, I nearly doubled that business. Fast forward three years later, and I had more than quadrupled it.

More senior lawyers and law firms need to take a lesson from my experience here. Diversity impacted the bottom line here in a big way. I was able to make headway with our urban school district clients that she had not been able to make as a white female. I took a slice of the pie and grew it exponentially so it impacted the profits of our entire group. In no time at all, we went from a small practice of three partners and one paralegal, to five partners, one of counsel, three associates, and multiple paralegals.

It was there I learned to help manage a practice group, make rain, train new lawyers, and all the other skills that are necessary as a full-fledged partner. As a senior female lawyer, I was especially cognizant of my role in helping to mentor and develop younger female attorneys. I could not and would not pull up the ladder as others were climbing behind me. After a while, I found I had more passion for doing this and left the practice of law altogether.

I spent almost four years as the director of strategic initiatives at an AmLaw 100 firm where I was formally responsible for developing diversity programming in seven US offices and two international offices, and where my innovative professional development programs for diverse lawyers were emulated and ultimately impacted how all firm lawyers were recruited, hired, developed, and promoted.

Approaching Law Firm Diversity Strategically and Creatively

I was recruited by my current firm, Ogletree Deakins, three years ago. At Ogletree, I now have formal responsibility for and lead a combined talent management and diversity and inclusion department. Today, I am responsible for over 700 lawyers in forty-seven offices in five countries.

Ogletree believes that teaching lawyers how to be culturally competent and inclusive is a vital professional development skill necessary to their success in an ever-evolving global marketplace. Ogletree's model of combining both lawyer professional development and diversity and inclusion efforts is a best practice that has proven to be very effective and should be followed by other law firms. One, it ensures that diversity and inclusion are integrated as a major strategic imperative for the firm and not siloed as a stand-alone effort, as is the case in many other firms. As such, the firm ensures there is diverse representation in the professional development programming offered to its lawyers, whether it be legal writing, business development coaching and training, or leadership development programming.

Two, to the extent that diverse groups or individuals in the firm need different or more specific customized training to meet their professional development needs, there is an expert firm resource to address that need. Three, having one department serve as the resource to both diverse and majority attorneys helps the firm to be able to more swiftly and deftly detect, address, and solve gaps in attorney development. Programs, initiatives, and/or policies can be developed, revised, or shuttered as a result of noted trends and best practices.

Ogletree's decision to fully staff and fund a Professional Development and Inclusion (PDI) Department is another best practice other law firms should implement. In just three years, this department has grown from a director, manager, and administrative assistant to a director, two managers, two coordinators, and two administrative assistants. It is one thing to say diversity is a core value, and it is quite another to provide core resources to demonstrate that value.

Over the past four years, Ogletree, through the PDI Department, has created the infrastructure for a fully operational and transformative program. Shortly after joining the firm in September 2011, the department carried out in-person interviews of attorneys in twenty-one offices, at every level and in every demographic, as a springboard to develop a PDI needs assessment/climate survey.

Interviews with over a hundred lawyers at Ogletree contributed to devising an appropriate survey instrument and creating a baseline of accurate information needed to build an effective, sustainable PDI plan. Given that 86 percent of Ogletree lawyers participated in the survey, the results provided a thorough picture of the strengths and challenges within the firm in these two critical areas and allowed the department to create a coordinated, strategic approach to diversity as a business imperative, including integrating that approach in the firm's professional development programs and overall firm strategy.

Accordingly, the 2012–2014 PDI Strategic Action Plan identified specific initiatives in hiring, promotion, development, and advancement of Ogletree's attorneys. It incorporated methods, programs, and best practices that have consistently shown superior results in top-ranked law firms nationwide. Pursuant to the plan, the PDI Department created the administrative and operational infrastructure needed to implement substantive initiatives throughout its forty-plus offices nationwide, which included overhauling the existing diversity committee and creating a smaller, more nimble steering committee of influential shareholders, creating a new professional development committee, creating an ambassador network of committed attorneys in each office for each steering committee, conducting bias training for all lawyers, creating three affinity groups, establishing systems to consistently track and report diversity metrics, and developing substantive programming for our top-performing lawyers, among many other things.

Now that a strong foundation has been laid, the PDI Department, with the guidance of its steering committees and under the leadership of the firm's Board of Directors, has established a new three-year strategic plan for 2015–2017. We will be focused on creating a professional development framework and learning management system to make the path to success at the firm clearer, not only for diverse attorneys, but for all lawyers.

We will roll out labor and employment benchmarks, develop a core competency framework that will be integrated into our recruiting, hiring, development, and evaluation systems, as well as develop quality substantive programming for the firm's new affinity groups. Moreover, we will continue to offer innovative leadership development and business growth/client development programming.

Conclusion

Looking ahead, our firm will continue to make significant progress in both professional development and diversity and inclusion, not only because we have committed the necessary resources to do so, but because we recognize how very vital both are to the firm's future growth and success. Culturally competent lawyers who are subject matter experts invested in their own and their client's success is a win-win in an increasingly diverse and global consumer market.

And I will continue to do my part to ensure that my unique personal and professional experiences and differences are brought to bear in this process. My past has certainly prepared me. I know now that every time I covered who I really was and every single micro-inequity I have endured because of my intersecting identities has prepared me for this work as Ogletree's first PDI director. I will leverage my past experiences to continue to create transformative, impactful initiatives. For this, I am grateful.

Key Takeaways

- Diverse lawyers must cultivate a mindset of persistence and positivity. Diverse lawyers should shun a "victim" mentality and refuse to allow their personal or professional circumstances to limit their aspirations or squelch their confidence.
- Diverse lawyers should strive to be authentic and leverage their differences, not "cover" them.
- Diverse lawyers need to work for as many partners as possible, never giving one person power over their career.

- Law firms need to provide diverse lawyers with mentors who do not have to be the same sex and/or race as well as sponsors who are willing to invest in their development and put their reputations on the line to help them succeed.

- Law firms must create strong onboarding programs to fully integrate diverse lawyers into the firm's fabric and ensure that developmental opportunities are equitably dispersed early in their career.

- Law firm partners need to give ongoing critical feedback to diverse lawyers to help them develop and grow, and let diverse lawyers know when they are top performers.

- Law firm partners must provide diverse lawyers with feedback outside of the formal evaluation process. By encouraging diverse lawyers to take ownership of their careers and engage in a "feed forward" process, diverse lawyers can seek the critical developmental advice from partners that they need to grow and develop.

- Law firms' professional development resources should be focused primarily on top-performing attorneys.

Michelle P. Wimes serves as the director of professional development and inclusion at Ogletree Deakins Nash Smoak & Stewart PC, one of the nation's largest labor and employment law firms. In her role, she leads the firm's efforts to attract, develop, retain, promote, and advance a diverse group of attorneys across the firm's national platform of forty-seven offices in the United States, Europe, Latin America, and the Caribbean. Additionally, she leads the firm's attorney training and professional development efforts. She is based in Ogletree Deakins' Kansas City office.

Dedication: *It is not easy finding the time to write in the midst of raising three wonderfully talented but super busy children, holding down my day job, and being a wife to a very busy husband who has his own flourishing career. So, I must thank my husband, Brian C. Wimes, for stepping up and handling soccer carpool, volleyball practices, and track meets while I strove to find time in the wee hours of the morning or late evenings to write this chapter. I also want to thank my daughter, Gabrielle, who listened to me read this chapter and offered her critical, keen input. Moreover, I have several colleagues who supported me through this process and offered their invaluable advice, including Laura Rogora, Sisi Hannibal, Michelle T. Johnson, Maria North Morgan, Vickie Yarbrough, and Werten Bellamy. These people are my personal and professional Board of Directors, and I am grateful for them. Finally, I want to thank my mother, Marilyn Scott, who continues to be my daily inspiration for persistence and positivity.*

Establishing Diversity at a Law Firm

Donna Burns
Human Resources Director
Chambliss Bahner and Stophel PC

ASPATORE

Introduction

Establishing diversity in a law firm or any corporate culture is an intentional process. Individual employees contribute in many different ways and bring value to the firm because of their differences. It is important to leverage all differences to maximize the potential rewards to the firm.

The process starts with defining diversity as it relates to the firm's mission and guiding principles, and then creating awareness and buy-in from the top down about the importance of diversity to achieving business success and a competitive advantage.

Defining Diversity within the Firm

In a law firm, diversity needs to be defined to include all differences, whether individual or organizational, that impact productivity and output of legal services. In addition to the product of expert legal advice and advocacy, clients also require other services that are supportive to the process and development of the end legal product. Non-attorneys who provide support to the legal services of the attorney can be critical to client satisfaction. Taking a team approach to provide service can produce the best end result for the client in a timely and more cost-efficient manner. From a client perspective, it gives the firm a more client-friendly, accessible image when they notice they have a cohesive team of both attorneys and non-attorneys with respect for each other providing multiple layers of support. The reality is that we may never fully utilize all of the unique skills available to the firm because we may not intentionally seek them out. Because law firms are focused on the services provided by lawyers, there may be many untapped skills that non-attorneys can offer, which go unrecognized or underdeveloped. Collaboration with non-attorney staff on strategic planning initiatives and looking for their input on operational efficiencies could improve business development and cut operational costs. These are therefore missed opportunities to add value to the firm.

It is important to recognize and respect the contributions of all employees at all levels and from all backgrounds. Everyone at the firm needs to embrace this idea for the firm to be successful. Top-level leadership must champion this philosophy as an overarching expectation and continuously reinforce this value in explicit ways. Promoting this philosophy in a corporate mission statement and holding attorneys and non-attorneys accountable helps reinforce this notion and embeds it into the culture. There is value in differences, thus diversity means appreciating these differences, including all characteristics and experiences that define each employee (attorney or non-attorney) and creating an environment of inclusiveness. This inclusion drives the firm to be more productive, innovative, and creative in meeting the needs of their clients. Diversity also includes appreciating differences in thinking, working, learning, and communicating with each other. Firms have to be strategic and intentional about diversity and ask, "Who is not at the table? Who is not being heard?" Otherwise, there will be exclusion of those who may be underrepresented and yet able to add value to the firm.

The Rewards of Diversity

Being a diverse law firm helps better represent the various communities within which the firm is doing business. If the firm demographics are similar to the communities where the firm does business, it attracts more business to the firm. The firm is able to quickly adapt and appreciate the needs of clients. Among the demographic trends law firms are probably aware of are: the consistent growth in the number of women in the workforce and women-owned businesses; the increase of immigrants in the workplace and foreign-owned businesses; and the changes in workplace values and the increasing need for work/life balance.

Diversity also helps the firm attract and retain talent that is representative of a multicultural workforce. Commitment to a diverse workforce helps the firm better understand their clients and become better equipped to provide effective, comprehensive services. Further, diversity helps the firm attract high-quality talent, foster stronger employee retention, and ensure that the firm has a positive work environment. It helps the firm become an employer of choice where employees want to stay and continue to develop along with it.

Climate Control: Tolerance and Diversity

Management has to begin with a vision for diversity. This should be defined as a first step and then build a mission statement to support the vision. Start with a vision of where the firm would like to be (e.g., to be recognized as an outstanding place for our owners and employees to work, with a commitment to ethics, service, community, and diversity…). Key people within the firm should be leading the charge and demonstrating that they embrace the vision. The mission statement should be in line with the overall corporate mission statement and incorporate the vision of the firm. For example, the mission statement for our firm is "To practice our profession so that our clients value us for our service and advice; our colleagues outside the firm respect us for our ability and integrity; and our colleagues within the firm regard us with trust and appreciation." The firm's diversity statement was then developed in support of the mission statement: "We recognize that differences in cultural backgrounds, experiences, and perspectives strengthen collaboration, increase innovation, and improve efficiency. Our commitment to diversity ensures that we have a positive work environment, encourages employee retention, and enables us to provide a more well-rounded approach to legal services."

Create a diversity committee combining key leadership, associate-level attorneys, and staff, working together to define the diversity vision and articulate the mission and objectives of the firm. While this effort needs to have the backing and support of senior leadership, it is most important to have all levels of the firm involved with the work of the committee. The diversity committee is charged with assessing the firm's needs and developing solutions with a strategic approach. The committee can recommend policies and plans to address areas where diversity can be improved. Once the recommendations/plans are implemented, the committee should continuously monitor and evaluate progress toward diversity goals.

Demonstrate support for community pipeline initiatives to grow the numbers of minorities and women in the legal field, beginning as early as middle school. There are many community career education initiatives already available in most communities that would welcome participation from lawyers and others in the legal field to educate young people and assist them in making career choices. Many young people have not considered the legal profession as a career that would be available or accessible to them. Mentoring and supporting young people as they move toward college will increase opportunities to recruit these same young people to work at the firm as they enter and move through law school.

Steps Along the Road to Diversity

Establish practices and policies that support and promote diversity at the firm, including:

- Intentionally recruiting from minority law schools and participating in career fairs to give candidates access to the firm. Use multiple sources for candidate recruitment, and routinely update job descriptions. Detailed job descriptions should be maintained on positions to recruit the right talent for each position. Have a policy of hiring only after you have had an opportunity to review a diverse candidate slate, helping to ensure that you have been open to all potential candidates.

- Establish a policy that allows practice heads to review assignments and ensure that key assignments are offered to women and minorities. Also, ensure that committee assignments and leadership opportunities are provided to everyone.

- Practice including mentoring programs for career development. Formalize mentoring programs to provide more opportunities to develop skills. Formal mentoring can help ensure success of younger attorneys.

- Support affinity groups (women, minority groups, LGBT groups, etc.). Affinity groups can help employees work through and address issues particular to them and can provide support and guidance on things that may not be evident or go unmentioned otherwise. Firms can offer leadership or other targeted training for affinity groups when the group has identified their needs. Affinity groups can also provide the informal mentoring. Networking events with the firm's female attorneys and female clients can help develop business as well as foster client confidence in the firm.

- A firm's commitment to flexible working arrangements can assist in recruiting and retaining talent. Having the appropriate balance between work and life is a must in today's world. There is no reason telecommuting and flexible working hours cannot be effective. Coming in for a set schedule each day is not always necessary, and if employees can work where and whenever they need to, so much more can be accomplished.

- Demonstrating and promoting community service in the community where the firm does business. Genuine concern for the community is demonstrated through commitment to professional and civic involvement. This commitment needs to be an expectation of everyone who works at the firm at any level. It is not only the "right thing to do," but it also reflects the firm's value in being a responsible contributor to the community it serves. Providing opportunities for employees at all levels to spend time contributing to the community is important to this effort.

- Ongoing diversity orientation and diversity training, including awareness and sensitivity training to create a common language and understanding and training related to firm policies and expectations. A strategic plan for diversity training needs to be developed, implemented, and evaluated. Identify the diversity champions at the firm early in the process to lead communication and the business case for ongoing training and awareness. Champions have to be able to tell anyone with questions why it is important to the firm and the benefits for the business. Framers of the training should be asking what are the hopes and goals for diversity and inclusion, and then determine a strategic plan to help the firm reach those goals.

Support from the Top

Visible support of diversity initiatives and goals from partners and key leadership of the firm is absolutely necessary to succeed. Training should be supported at the highest levels of the firm. Key firm leaders should be out in front of diversity training and promoting it for everyone with a message articulating the firm's purpose for conducting training and mandate to participate.

Hopefully, high-level leadership at the firm is actively involved with the diversity committee and supportive of the training needs. It is important that key leadership be involved in setting the stage for training and kicking off the initiative. When the diversity statement is defined and strategy for training developed, it is important to have partner buy-in to establish commitment. To ensure buy-in at this level, there has to be a shared need established among partners by communicating a meaningful business case for diversity. For most firms, the business case is described in terms of clients, and client demand can be a key driver. However, there are many other competitive reasons that may support the business case for diversity. Presenting the tangible benefits of diversity to partners will emphasize this point. This may include some of the following:

- The composition of the communities where the firm does business is changing.
- Corporations and clients are becoming increasingly diverse and expect this from their vendors and partners.
- Corporations are demanding it of their law firms.
- Diversity creates a stronger workforce.

Assess, Define, Train

It is necessary to be strategic with training and address where the firm is currently and then assess where it needs to be. This begins with a formal firm definition of diversity and a clear vision and policy statement that is custom-fitted to the needs and challenges of the firm. The diversity statement should build from the mission and philosophy of the firm and be communicated to all employees of the firm on a regular basis.

Formulating the firm's diversity statement should be a task of the diversity committee and involve all levels of the firm. Development of the diversity statement can take some time and debate, but it is important in leading your training plan. Our diversity committee began with a vision statement that was simply focused on making the firm an outstanding place to work and reviewed how this vision translated to our mission statement and guiding values. We began reminding employees in staff meetings and internal publications what our mission and values were because they were actually directly in line with our commitment to diversity. Once that was clearly articulated, we began crafting a diversity statement from the perspective of the diversity committee members. Developing a consensus statement took several meetings and revisions, but once that was accomplished we were able to meet with all employees and roll out the vision and statement and begin the plan for awareness training.

There are different levels of training that should be considered. Awareness training is probably the best place to begin and provides participants with a realistic look from the firm's perspective at what diversity means and the various aspects of diversity that make up the firm's identity. It is not just about race or gender. Awareness and inclusion is about all of the things that contribute to the firm's diversity, including differences in background, behavioral differences, and differences in working and thinking.

Awareness Training

Level one awareness training can lay the groundwork for awareness and dialogue and can include:

- Answering the questions: "What is diversity?" "Why does the firm care about having a diverse workforce?" "What does diversity bring to the firm?"
- Provide an overview of the firm vision and commitment to diversity.
- Present the firm's diversity strategy.
- Introduce the firm's intention to provide ongoing awareness training.

These topics can get everyone thinking about diversity in similar ways and prepare participants for the next level of training, which should take a deeper look at how the firm intends to be inclusive and what types of skills may be necessary to achieve that inclusiveness. Most people do not intend to be exclusive, but awareness of behaviors and how they may be interpreted by others helps bring that to their awareness.

Level two awareness training objectives include:

- Raise awareness and create a common language on the topic of diversity and inclusion.
- Recognize inclusive and exclusive behaviors.
- Provide attorneys and employees with the behavioral skills to interact with co-workers of varying backgrounds, cultures, and life experiences.

Diversity training can be intimidating for some. Most people expect that it will be all about "lecturing," and they will not expect to get much from the training session. Plus they may have some barriers up that need to be overcome to get the real message across. Thus, training should be conducted in a "safe" atmosphere that is supportive and non-judgmental. In most cases, an external trainer/facilitator that is well regarded in this field, with lots of experience, will be better received than any internal training option. Diversity trainers need to be "right" for the firm and fit with the firm objectives for training. Training has to be engaging, fun, and memorable. It takes unique skills to make participants feel at ease.

We recently used an external facilitator who was well regarded and had the credentials to support his ability on the topic of diversity. He started his sessions by stating he was "suspending all political correctness" and encouraged participants to share their comments and questions without the "correctness" filter. This actually helped ease a lot of tension on the topic and manage the resistance in the room. However, it takes special skills to be capable of facilitating this level of discussion on a topic that can be sensitive to many people.

Effectiveness

It is important to be as successful as possible when initiating training. Measurement of the effectiveness of training is critical to continuing the training. After training sessions, participants should complete evaluation forms to provide feedback on what worked well with the training and if it accomplished the intended goals. It also provides feedback on additional topics that should be addressed in future training and adjustments to methodology to achieve optimum results.
Training has to be a priority in the overall diversity plan. It is an investment that takes time, constant attention, and resources to be effective.

Conclusion

In the end, diversity and inclusion is about becoming more productive, innovative, and creative as a firm. However, diversity is complex and it can be difficult to stay focused with so many pressing issues that compete for the firm's attention. Take it in small steps and embrace the process. To be successful, it is necessary to develop a shared vision that is communicated across the firm in a meaningful way to engage everyone and continually point to the tangibles that diversity brings to the firm.

Key Takeaways

- Support the overall success of the firm by learning to seek out and utilize the unique skills available to the firm among all the levels, partners and associates, lawyers and non-lawyers. Avoid focusing solely on services provided by lawyers, and learn to recognize and respect the contributions of all employees at all levels and from all backgrounds. Make it a policy from the top down to appreciate the various characteristics and experiences defining each employee, resulting in a firm that is more productive, innovative, and creative in meeting the needs of clients.

- Build the diversity committee from all levels within the firm: leadership, associate-level attorneys, and staff. The first task is to define the diversity vision and articulate the mission and objectives of the firm. Then assess the firm's needs and develop solutions with a strategic approach, followed by recommending policies and plans to address areas where diversity can be improved. The job does not end there, but the committee should be charged with continuous monitoring and evaluation of the progress toward diversity goals.

- Intentionally recruit from minority law schools and participate in career fairs to give candidates access to the firm. Use multiple sources for candidate recruitment and routinely update job descriptions. Maintain detailed job descriptions to recruit the right talent for each position.

Donna Burns is a human resources director at Chambliss Bahner and Stophel PC, where she oversees the firm's Human Resources Division, managing employee relations, benefits administration, performance management, recruiting, and staffing for all permanent and temporary positions, initiating and implementing all firm policies, and supervising a wide variety of related matters. She joined the firm in 2007 with twelve years of progressive experience in human resources management.

Ms. Burns has more than fifteen years of experience in training development and delivery, and she worked directly with community service programs to enhance career development for disadvantaged populations. She is a Certified Senior Professional in Human Resources.

APPENDICES

APPENDIX A

THE FMLA AND SAME-SEX MARRIED COUPLES

On February 25, 2015, the US Department of Labor (DOL) finalized a new rule (which was published in the *Federal Register*) expanding protections under the Family and Medical Leave Act (FMLA) for same-sex married couples.

The FMLA provides twelve weeks of job-protected leave for eligible employees and can be used to care for a spouse with a serious health condition. Currently, same-sex couples qualify for such FMLA protection only if the state where they live recognizes their marriage. When the new rule takes effect on March 27, 2015, all married same-sex couples will be entitled to FMLA protection, regardless of whether their home state recognizes their marriage.

The new DOL regulation will redefine "spouse" to include "the other person with whom an individual entered into marriage as defined or recognized under state law for purposes of marriage in the state in which the marriage was entered into." This means that a same-sex couple's marriage must be lawfully recognized where it was performed—either abroad or in one of the thirty-seven states that has legalized same-sex marriage—for the couple to be covered by the FMLA. It will no longer matter whether their marriage is legal where they reside.

Employers in states that have not legalized same-sex marriage will need to be prepared for a potential uptick in FMLA leave applications after the rule takes effect in March. The new regulation is unlikely to result in significant changes for employers in states that have legalized same-sex marriage.

See more at: http://blog.ogletreedeakins.com/same-sex-spouses-to-be-covered-by-fmla-as-of-march-27-2015/?sthash.OE4xZWXM.mjjo# sthash.OE4xZWXM.kFBSYhOr.dpuf

Courtesy of Michelle Wimes, Ogletree Deakins Nash Smoak & Stewart PC

APPENDIX B

VISIBLE INVISIBILITY: WOMEN OF COLOR IN FORTUNE 500 LEGAL DEPARTMENTS

Executive Summary

The story of women of color in the legal profession is multi-layered and deeply rooted in the broader societal issues related to racial, ethnic, and gender equality that have existed in the United States since this country's inception. Their story has been no fairy tale, and, so far, female attorneys of color are not living happily ever after. To the contrary, theirs has been and continues to be a narrative of struggle against marginalization, low expectations, and gross inequity, which, arguably, has rendered them second-class citizens in their chosen profession. Women of color stand as a visible and living embodiment of not only the natural ethnic and gender differences that exist between human beings but also of the artificial racial constructs that divide and separate. Their double minority status shades their experiences. The story of female attorneys of color has been told from a variety of perspectives, but its ending has yet to be written.

Female attorneys of color have made undeniable inroads into the leadership ranks of a number of Fortune 500 law departments. A small group of diverse female attorneys have reached the upper echelons of corporate legal practice. In 2005, there were only five women of color general counsel. In 2010, there were 17 (approximately 3.41 percent of all Fortune 500 general counsels and 18.1 percent of the total number of women holding such positions). Despite these positive signs of forward movement, the majority of female attorneys of color continue to face barriers that thwart their ability to achieve their full potential. Unfortunately, female attorneys of color are more likely than other groups to be sidetracked by obstacles that limit their opportunities for success early on in their careers. For example, female attorneys of color:

- Have the highest attrition rate of any group of attorneys[1]
- Are more likely than any other group to experience exclusion from other employees based on racial and gender stereotyping;[2]
- Are most likely to feel the need to make adjustments to fit into the workplace;[3] and
- Are more likely to cite dissatisfaction with current levels of work and access to high-profile client assignments relative to experience.[4]

The American Bar Association (ABA) and its constituent entities continue to work tirelessly to effect the change that will eventually eradicate the inequities that disproportionately impact diverse and underrepresented groups in society at large. The ABA Commission on Women in the Profession, through its Women of Color Research Initiative, is contributing to this effort by giving female attorneys of color a platform from which to tell their unique stories, in their own words. This groundbreaking project was designed to:

- Shine an unforgiving light on the inequities affecting female attorneys of color, particularly in the areas of compensation and career advancement;

---

[1] Diversity and Flexibility Connection—Best Practices (The Project for Attorney Retention and the Minority Corporate Counsel Association), at 3 (Oct. 29, 2009) (http://www.attorneyretention.org/Publications/DiverFlexConn_BestPractices.pdf);see also Minority Corporate Counsel Association (MCCA), The Myth of the Meritocracy: A Report on the Bridges and Barriers to Success in Large Law Firms, "Different Experiences," at 33 (Purple Book) (available at www.mcca.com).

[2] ABA Commission on Women in the Profession, Visible Invisibility: Women of Color in Law Firms at 9 (2006) (www.americanbar.org/groups/women/initiatives_awards/women_of_color_research_initiative/2006wocannual.html). See also Catalyst, Women in Law in the U.S., at 4 (2010) (www.catalyst.org/publication/246/women-in-law-in-the-us); Women's Bar Association of the District of Columbia (WBADC), Initiative on Advancement and Retention of Women, Creating Pathways to Success for All: Advancing and Retaining Women of Color in Today's Law Firms (May 2008) (available at http://wba.timberlakepublishing.com/files/Advocacy%20&%20Endorsements%20Files/Initiative%20 Reports/Creating_Pathways_to_Success_for_All-March_2008.pdf).

[3] Visible Invisibility, supra note 2, at 9. See also Pathways to Success for All, supra note 2, at 9-11.

[4] Visible Invisibility, supra note 2, at 9. See also Women in Law, supra note 2, at 4; Pathways to Success for All, supra note 2, at 11.

- Identify the root causes of these inequities;
- Develop replicable strategies that women of color in all areas of the legal profession can use to advance their careers; and
- Offer practical suggestions and recommendations to legal employers across all sectors that will enable them to better address the needs of the diverse female attorneys they employ, which, ultimately, will enhance their retention of these attorneys.

In phase I of the Women of Color Research Initiative, the Commission examined the diversity dynamics of female attorneys of color in law firm settings. The findings of this study are detailed in the 2006 report entitled, Visible Invisibility: Women of Color in Law Firms.[5] This phase focuses on the experiences of women of color in corporate law departments.

Women of color bear what some describe as "dual burdens" of minority status. The goal of this and the Commission's 2006 study is to elicit data specific to the impact that race/ethnicity and gender have on the career mobility of female attorneys of color, particularly in relation to recruitment, hiring, retention, and advancement. In fact, it is the cyclical and interdependent relationships among these four major aspects of an attorney's career that are the central focus of this report. Female attorneys of color are caught in a Catch-22 of sorts: they have to be recruited, hired, and retained to advance to leadership positions. Yet, without significant female attorneys of color already in leadership to help pave the way, organizations are not always ready to facilitate such advancement. Therein lies the challenge before us—growing and developing the number of female attorneys of color from entry-level to leadership positions.

This phase of the ABA Commission on Women in the Profession's initiative takes an in-depth look at the career experiences of women of color in relation to the experiences of their white male, white female, and men of

---

[5] Visible Invisibility, supra note 2. The Commission published a second report detailing the experiences of 28 successful women lawyers of color and their recommendations for achieving success. Commission, From Visible Invisibility to Visibly Successfully: Success Strategies for Law Firms and Women of Color in Law Firms (2007) (www.americanbar.org/groups/women/initiatives_awards/women_of_color_research_init itaive_vsendorsers. html).

color counterparts in corporate legal settings. The Commission's study of the combined impact of race, ethnicity, and gender on the career mobility of women of color in law firm and law department settings has produced a plethora of data on the subject. Building on the work of other organizations, the Commission's Women of Color Research Initiative has worked to develop a comparative study that will be the most comprehensive, systematic, and authoritative research conducted on the subject to date. The goal is to examine the underlying systemic and cultural factors that continue to prevent female attorneys of color from achieving their full potential, and to identify practical and accessible solutions that can be applied across all legal practice sectors.

How does the Commission accomplish this? For starters the right questions must be asked: Is there a difference in success for women of color in corporate law departments measured both quantitatively and qualitatively, compared to white men, white women, and men of color? How do women of color compare their experiences in corporate law departments to those of white men, white women, and men of color? How much of their experience can be attributed to race, ethnicity, gender, or a combination thereof? What are the retention and attrition rates for women of color in corporate law departments, and what are the factors that cause women of color to leave? Are the reasons that cause women of color to leave different from those of white men, white women, or men of color? What strategies do women of color in corporate law departments use that lead to career success? Do these strategies differ from those of white men, white women, and men of color? And finally, how do the answers to these questions compare to those of female attorneys of color in law firms, as explored in our previous study?

Methodology

The current phase of the Commission's Research Initiative explores the diversity dynamics of female attorneys of color in Fortune 500 law departments. It is based on the results of a national online survey of more than 1,000 respondents conducted from October 2010 through February 2011. The survey targeted a broad cross-section of both current and former Fortune 500 in-house attorneys of both genders and all racial and ethnic backgrounds, which enabled the Commission to draw out a range of perspectives and experiences. The survey responses provided both quantitative and qualitative information on how the confluence of gender, race, and ethnicity affects the work lives of female attorneys of color in corporate law departments. The final version of the survey consisted of 52 questions that were designed to elicit responses on a variety of topics. The Commission on Women engaged the services of Nextions (formerly The Athens Group), a nationally-recognized, Chicago-based firm specializing in diversity and inclusion strategic consulting, leadership development, and executive coaching, to conduct the underlying research for this study.

The survey sample was self-selected; thus, the respondents were not randomly chosen to participate. The total number of respondents in the survey sample who identified their gender was 784: 577 (74 percent) women and 207 (26 percent) men. Many of the survey respondents disclosed their race or ethnicity but some did not, making it impossible to determine exact percentage breakdowns of these subsets within the broad gender categories noted above. However, based on the demographic information obtained from those respondents who chose to self-identify, it is known that at least 386 were white women, 186 were women of color, 155 were white men, and 50 were men of color.[6] In short, 541 were white attorneys and 236 were attorneys of color.

Summary of Findings

The survey responses, in many ways, confirmed what the Commission, from its previous work on these issues, already suspected—that female attorneys of color in the corporate sector face many of the same issues and obstacles as their women of color counterparts in law firms, including the negative impact of bias and stereotypes on their careers. Survey responses were varied and often fell along racial, ethnic, and/or gender lines. However, in a few instances, no discernible experiential difference between groups was found.

---

[6] The sample size of the men of color participating in the Fortune 500 law department study is small relative to the number of women of color, white women, and white men surveyed. Given the self-selected nature of the survey, this type of statistical anomaly can be expected. Notwithstanding the limited representation of men of color in the research sample, the overall methodology of the study is reliable, and the quantitative and qualitative data derived from the survey offers valuable insight into the experiences of the representative groups surveyed, including men of color.

Relative to the issue of mentoring, for example, 18 percent of women of color and 19 percent of white males reported that they had no formal mentors. The underlying reasons for their lack of mentors varied. Women of color were more likely to be without a mentor due to an inability to establish relationships with senior attorneys, who are overwhelmingly white males. White men were more likely to be without a mentor due to a belief that they could succeed on their own and did not need a mentor to advance.

However, the survey responses also highlighted some distinctions between the experiences of female attorneys of color in law firms and those in the corporate arena, including greater overall job satisfaction and improved (though not perfect) work-life balance and integration policies for women of color in-house. The majority of the women of color surveyed in the law department study believed that their experiences of career-related bias are based on the combination of racial, ethnic, and gender factors. Of all of the groups surveyed, women of color reported the most consistent levels of discrimination across race, ethnicity, and gender. They were more likely to report higher levels of discrimination based on race and/or ethnicity than their white counterparts and greater levels of gender bias than their male colleagues.

As was the case in the Commission's law firm study, the majority of the women of color participating in the law department survey reported a negligible influence of overt bias at the recruitment and hiring stages. Respondents in both studies reported a more insidious influence of bias during the mid- to later stages of their careers. This is particularly true for women of color, who have the highest attrition rate of all groups surveyed. Recruitment is the first step in developing a strong talent pool of attorneys of color. As a threshold issue, unfortunately, the pipeline into the profession has become increasingly less diverse in the last 10 years. The number of women and minorities entering law school has dwindled significantly, resulting in a diminished pool of diverse candidates eligible for recruitment into the profession. The tepid economy has further debilitated what was already a weak stream of minorities and women primed and ready to move into entry-level legal positions.

Minority attorneys currently comprise only 10 percent of the legal profession. What is turning diverse attorneys, particularly women of color, away from the profession? Some argue that women's slow rate of progress in reaching leadership levels may deter young women of color from enrolling in law school. Others argue that disparities in compensation between male and female attorneys—which can result in a cumulative difference of $2 million over the course of a lawyer's career—have discouraged women of color from choosing law as a career.

Women of color in corporate law departments are the least likely of all groups to be hired at top executive or senior management levels and the most likely to be hired at junior levels. Commensurately, women of color are most likely to be hired at salary scales lower than their white female and all male counterparts, across almost all pay categories.

Retention

Law firms especially struggle with retaining diverse attorneys. In fact, retention of talented minorities has proven to be the most problematic phase of the career continuum for women of color, as evidenced by their extraordinarily high attrition rate from law firms. Women of color make up 17 percent of associates who left their firms in their third year.[7] Aside from not feeling valued and appreciated, women of color leave law firms for a variety of reasons, including not feeling supported (22 percent), the inability to establish mentorship relationships (21 percent), feeling isolated and marginalized (16 percent), and being subjected to stereotypes and discrimination (11 percent).[8] Corporate law departments have been able to capitalize on this dissatisfaction and have successfully lured away record numbers of women of color who are looking for opportunities to advance their careers in more welcoming environments than those law firms have been able to offer.

---

[7] Recession's Impact on Minorities at Law Firms: Anomaly or Trend (Oct. 4, 2010) (http://www.lawschoolpodcaster.com/2010/10/04/recessions-impact-on-minorities-atlaw-firms-anomaly-or-trend/).

[8] What Female Attorneys of Color Want, Black Enterprise (July 2011)(www.blackenterprise.com) (also available at www.ccwomenofcolor.org/press/Black_Enterprise_7-11.pdf). See also Visible Invisibility, supra note 2, at 30-35 (discussing job satisfaction); Pathways to Success for All, supra note 2, at 8-9.

The women of color surveyed highlighted some positive distinctions between their experiences in law firms and in corporate law departments, including the:

- Opportunity offered by their corporate law departments to broaden their expertise beyond the law into the business side of their companies;
- Ability to develop more intimate, meaningful relation-ships with clients; and
- Opportunity to escape the pressures of stringent billable hours requirements and establish a better work-life balance.

Although most were pleased with their decision to leave law firms for in-house practice, women of color reported being less satisfied with their decision than their white counterparts. Seventeen percent of female attorneys of color reported that they were extremely satisfied with their decision to work for a Fortune 500 company, compared to 48 percent of white males. Fourteen percent of women of color reported that they were satisfied with their decision to work for a Fortune 500 company, compared to 37 percent of white males. Eleven percent of women of color reported being dissatisfied with their decision to move in-house, compared to just 7 percent of white males.

According to survey responses, female attorneys of color were more likely than white male attorneys to leave their Fortune 500 law departments to gain greater experience and to obtain better work-life integration. The disparity in these statistics points to a fundamental difference in the experience of female attorneys of color and their white counterparts.

Respondents in both the Commission's law firm and law department studies noted the difficult choices and trade-offs that attorneys have to make to achieve a reasonable balance between their professional and personal lives. Concerns about, and dissatisfaction with, quality of life issues drove many of the respondents in the current study to leave their law firms for in-house jobs. The flexibility in scheduling and reduced pressure to meet billable hours requirements offered by in-house work enable women, particularly female attorneys of color, to better manage child care and other family-related obligations. Women of color have long had to deal with the misperception that they leave law firms because they want to avoid hard work. On the contrary, they are seeking ways to work smarter— ways that will enable them to have fulfilling careers without neglecting their families. Legal employers that offer female attorneys of color greater options in developing and advancing their careers without shortchanging their familial obligations will ultimately have greater success in retaining these employees (and others as well).

Survey respondents identified several factors that they believe would have a positive effect on their careers. Thirty-seven percent indicated that increased gender diversity would improve their career satisfaction. Twenty-three percent stated that more consistency in the implementation of alternative work policies would have a positive impact.

The respondents in our current study identified several problematic areas in corporate law departments, including limited or no access to networks (internal and external), unfair performance reviews, less-than-transparent promotion policies and procedures, disparity in pay, and the lack of mentors and sponsors willing to advocate on their behalf. The latter issues, compensation and mentoring and sponsorship, are issues that thread throughout a woman of color's career, from beginning to end. As can be expected, all play a significant role in determining career success and affecting lawyers' decisions to stay—or leave—their jobs.

Mentoring

The difficulty that women of color encounter in building professional relationships affects their careers in profoundly negative ways the further removed they are from law school. Women of color are often perceived as "flight risks"—not worth the investment of time and resources for career development. Ironically, it is this very type of investment that would most likely stem the tide of attrition among this group of attorneys. Moreover, women of color are more likely to come from less privileged and less moneyed backgrounds and are also more likely to be the first in their families to graduate college and law school. As a result, they often lack access to connections, support, and guidance from influential friends, family members, and business associates. Lack of access to these crucial career-enhancing relationships can mean the difference between career success and career stagnation.

Further, mentoring (or the lack thereof) can affect a lawyer's ability to navigate successfully other notable trouble spots that arise at the retention stage for female attorneys of color, including limited or no access to important networks, unfair performance evaluations, access to quality assignments, and denial of promotion opportunities. As was noted in the Commission's study of women of color in law firms, lack of access to networks, the inability to obtain quality work assignments, and limited opportunities for advancement may be the "critical differentiating factors in the careers of men and women, and especially women of color."

The women of color respondents in the Fortune 500 study were hungry for mentors who often did not materialize. Many respondents in the law department survey found formal mentoring programs to be ineffective. Twenty-five percent of female attorneys of color surveyed had formal mentors. Those who had formal mentors were less likely to have white male mentors, which, in effect, limited their access to the influential powerbrokers in their departments.

Most of the survey respondents regardless of race, ethnicity, or gender believed that they received the most beneficial mentoring through informal channels. Many indicated a preference for mentoring relationships that developed "naturally" over time rather than more "forced" relationships established via formal mentoring programs. Twenty-two percent of female attorneys of color reported having informal mentors. As was the case with formal mentoring, female attorneys of color were less likely to be informally mentored by white male attorneys.

Fortune 500 companies offer mentoring options that law firms do not, namely, the opportunity to develop relationships and form alliances with mentors on the business side of the company. These mentors can serve as outside advisors who can help protégés navigate politically sensitive situations. They can also assist protégés in broadening their knowledge about the non-legal, business end of the company, thus grooming them for corporate advancement. Women of color generally reported access to mentors but less ultimate career success, a finding indicating that, while women often have many mentors, they have few sponsors—the influential leaders who can help ensure promotion and maximum career success.

Complicating this scenario even more is the issue of compensation, which negatively impacts female attorneys of color at every juncture of their careers, in a variety of ways. The disparity between the salaries of male and female attorneys, particularly female attorneys of color, is compounded over time and affects not only base salary but bonuses, benefits, and retirement as well.

Fair and equitable pay is the clearest, strongest measurement of the value that an employer places on an attorney and her abilities. Thus, compensation is the prism through which bias—both overt and subtle—against female attorneys of color can be measured. Furthermore, it is the most obvious metric by which to effectively judge the progress being made toward the achievement of parity between female attorneys of color and their white male counterparts.

Disparities in compensation related to salary, bonuses, benefits, and retirement have a ripple effect on the recruitment, hiring, retention, and ultimate advancement of women and women of color attorneys, and contribute significantly to the high attrition rate among these groups. Female attorneys of color are at a distinct salary disadvantage from the day they accept their first job. This income disparity (typically a 25 percent difference between women of color and white men) grows disproportionately over the course of a lawyer's career. One study noted that "what starts as a $2,000 annual gap between male and female associates accelerates to a $66,000 annual gap between male and female equity partners."[9] Fairness issues related to pay can also have a negative impact on hiring, causing women of color to choose alternative employment where they feel more valued. Finally, the negative relationship between money and maternity cannot be dismissed, as having children does not disadvantage men; in addition, women of color are more likely than white women to be

---

[9] Forward by Roberta D. Liebenberg & Catherine L. Lamboley to report by Joan C. Williams & Veta T. Richardson, The Project for Attorney Retention, MCCA, and ABA, New Millennium, Same Glass Ceiling? The Impact of Law Firm Compensation Systems on Women (July 2010) (http://www.attorneyretention.org/Publications/SameGlass Ceiling.pdf). See also Martha Neil, Survey Finds "Deep Vein of Anger" Among Women Partners Over Law Firm Pay Gap (www.abajournal.com/news/article/survey_finds_ deep_vein_of_an-ger_among_women_partners_ove_lower_law_firm_pay).

sole breadwinners and typically come from less affluent backgrounds, have fewer resources, and face more demands on their finances and time.

As female attorneys of color move through their careers, compensation becomes a more critical issue. Further exacerbating the situation is the documented fact that women are less likely than men to negotiate salary. Women are often reluctant to ask for what they are worth for fear of being labeled "pushy," "demanding," or "aggressive." This reluctance puts them at a disadvantage relative to compensation. Female attorneys of color, who are generally the least supported of any group, are even more handicapped when it comes to salary negotiation. They are consistently at the bottom of the salary totem pole, despite the fact that they are disproportionately the sole breadwinners in their households, with more demands placed on their limited resources.

Unlike their white male counterparts, who also tend to be the sole breadwinners, female attorneys of color do not typically have the same level of spousal support to fall back on, particularly as it relates to child and elder care. Because they are often the sole or primary provider in their families, salary negotiation is a trickier, more delicate proposition for them. In addition to being saddled with negative labels, they often fear that, if they ask for "too much," they risk losing job opportunities that are essential to the support of their families. Likewise, they often have the fewest options to quit a professionally unrewarding job. This is an area where effective mentoring can make a meaningful difference but, unfortunately, is often lacking.

A good mentor will give his or her woman of color protégé the push needed to get to the next level through high-priority assignments and entrée into influential net-works, which will, in turn, enable her to receive positive performance reviews and promotions. A sponsor will help drive his or her protégé up the ladder of career success. Ultimately, this type of career development will help the protégé establish the necessary credentials to increase her value to potential employers. Moreover, female attorneys of color with these advantages will be better able to merchandise themselves successfully during job interviews and performance evaluations. Unfortunately, female attorneys of color rarely receive this type of guidance, significantly diminishing their chances for career and salary growth, and further sowing the seeds of discontent, which often lead to attrition.

Advancement

The high levels of attrition and entrenched problems with retention (including issues of tokenism, stereotypes, double standards, and perceptions of incompetence) have placed a stranglehold on the pipeline of diverse female attorneys feeding into the leadership ranks of the profession. Therefore, it should come as no surprise that the pool of female attorneys of color groomed to ascend to leadership is severely limited. This fact, coupled with historical problems with bias in the promotion process, has resulted in a dearth of female attorneys of color in positions of authority. Four percent of female attorneys of color reported being denied promotion or advancement due to race or ethnicity, compared to 1 percent of white male attorneys and male attorneys of color, and 0.6 per-cent of white female attorneys. Likewise, 4 percent of female attorneys of color reported being denied promotion or advancement based on gender, compared to 2 percent of white male attorneys, 0.1 percent of male attorneys of color, and 13 percent of white female attorneys.

Female attorneys of color reported more consistent levels of negative bias across racial, ethnic, and gender categories, further demonstrating the impact of these factors on their careers. The majority of respondents surveyed indicated that they would leave their employment with a Fortune 500 law department to obtain a salary increase and to take advantage of an advancement opportunity. Women of color reported a significant likelihood of leaving to avoid barriers to advancement (23 percent), obtain experience not otherwise available to them (19 percent), and take advantage of an advancement opportunity (18 percent).

Finally, as women of color seek promotion to leadership levels, the inextricable connection between compensation and advancement becomes even more evident. Compensation disparities at this level manifest themselves in the form of disputes over salary negotiation, transparency, and client succession. Women of color must be able to master the art of salary negotiation; otherwise, they stand to lose more than half a million dollars by the end of their professional careers.

Bias and Inequity in the Workplace

Workplace bias manifests itself in various ways.

Respondents indicated gender bias as the primary form of bias that affects their professional careers in all but one category. Women, more than their male counterparts, identified gender as having the greater negative influence on their careers in these categories. As one woman stated, "I have to work harder to make up for being a female." White women were more likely to indicate gender as the most prevalent form of bias affecting their careers in these categories. However, attorneys of color cited race and ethnicity as having greater negative effects on their careers than did non-minority respondents. Moreover, women of color were more likely consistently to report the negative effects of racial, ethnic, and gender bias combined across all bias categories. White male attorneys were most likely to report low levels of bias in these categories. For the most part, the respondents' perceptions of bias and the impact of bias on their careers cut across racial, ethnic, and gender lines.

Special Note on Bias: Reverse Discrimination

The report includes a Special Note on Bias addressing the topic of "reverse discrimination." A small number of respondents in the Commission's law department study raised the issue of diversity-based hiring practices as a form of reverse discrimination. This notion is based on the false assumption that diverse candidates are inherently less qualified and, conversely, that white males are inherently qualified. The data derived from both the Commission's law firm and law department studies, as well as other well-respected studies conducted on the topic, tell the story of the real and significant inequities that persist between minorities and non-minorities. These inequities belie the claims that women of color are reaping undeserved advantages at the expense of their white male counterparts.

Conclusion

The truth is that women of color face less fulfilling careers, with consistently lower compensation, bonuses, and benefits, and also direct and indirect racial, ethnic, and gender bias and stereotyping on a daily basis. The statistics do not lie:

- Women of color attorneys have the highest attrition rate of any group;
- Women of color attorneys lag well behind other groups in compensation from the beginning to the end of their careers; and
- Women of color attorneys have the least access to mentors and important networks that facilitate career development.

Corporate legal employers must be prepared to respond to claims of reverse discrimination in intelligent ways if they seek to prevent such claims from derailing diversity initiatives in their companies.

The Commission believes that this phase of the Women of Color Research Initiative will play a role in leveling the playing field for women of color working in-house. Given the influence that in-house counsel can have on law firms, the Commission also believes that the work of its Research Initiative can have a critical influence on improving retention and advancement of women of color in law firms.

The findings of this report indicate that many respondents left law firm practice for greater career satisfaction in-house. In-house lawyers hire outside law firms, thus providing corporate law departments with the opportunity to improve diversity not only within their own ranks but also among the law firms, and outside lawyers, they hire. Corporate law departments are in a unique position to insist that their outside counsel be represented by diverse teams of lawyers that include women of color and that these diverse lawyers receive the training, visibility, and origination and billing credit that will ensure their career success.

The substantial statistical and anecdotal data derived from the survey responses enables the Commission to compare and contrast the wide-ranging experiences of women of color. It is through these comparisons that the Commission is able to identify and isolate the hot-button issues affecting diverse women throughout the profession and, ultimately, to suggest strategies to ameliorate the disparities that continue to exist between women of color and their non-minority counterparts. The suggestions and recommendations that are offered here are intended as a jumping-off point for corporate legal employers who are serious about creating and maintaining a diverse and fully inclusive work environment that supports the unique needs of female attorneys of color. The strategies highlighted in this report are meant to elicit thoughtful, creative, and meaningful solutions to problems that have their roots in this nation's historical struggle with racism, sexism, and discrimination.

Women of color bear the brunt of dual minority status in significant ways. They are the repository for every stereotype, negative bias, and low expectation associated with race, ethnicity, and gender. More than any other group, their intellect, abilities, and professionalism are routinely questioned and second-guessed, often in the subtle and poorly understood ways that stereotyping, unexamined bias, and unearned privilege are expressed. Women of color are underdogs who, as the Commission's work has shown, are consistently underpaid, underestimated, and undervalued. Sadly, female attorneys of color often are treated as second-class citizens in a profession that ironically is charged with the responsibility of ensuring justice and equality for all.

Women of color are disproportionately more likely to be single parents, sole providers, with little or no back-up financial support and limited options for the significant demands arising from care of children and elderly parents. Due to these constraints, many feel that they have no choice but to suffer in silence in work environments that do not embrace their diversity. They are, in essence, trapped in dead-end positions that are essential to their livelihood but do not nourish their intellect or career aspirations. Moreover, female attorneys of color are at once visible and invisible. Their visibility breeds both contempt and subtle (and not so subtle) acts of discrimination, while their invisibility breeds neglect. Further, they must often contend with these issues alone, with no one to mentor them and advocate on their behalf. The ABA Commission on Women in the Profession joins those other organizations that have been working to champion the cause of female attorneys of color—to be their voice. The Commission's goal is to bring about the change in the profession that will finally level the playing field for women of color, putting them on a par with their non-diverse colleagues, both professionally and financially.

It is the Commission's hope that Fortune 500 law departments will use the information and comments provided throughout this comparative study as a guide to aid them in supporting female attorneys of color as they strive to reach their full potential. With thoughtful policies and commitment, corporate law departments can avoid the missteps of their law firm brethren, which have resulted in the attrition of significant numbers of disenchanted women of color. Instead, law departments must continue to maintain those areas that make them attractive to attorneys seeking an alternative to law firm life and strengthen those areas that the respondents in the study have identified as problematic. Furthermore, because of their unique relationship with outside counsel, law departments have an opportunity to positively influence law firms in their struggle to retain talented women and minorities. If law departments are able to do this, growing numbers of female attorneys of color will be seen in the partnership ranks of law firms and the general counsel suites of major Fortune 500 law departments in the very near future.

In 1994, the chief legal officers of approximately 500 major corporations signed their commitment to a document entitled, Diversity in the Workplace—A Statement of Principle.[10]10   Roderick Palmore, then Executive Vice President, General Counsel, and Secretary of Sara Lee, created the "Call to Action" initiative. In it, he asked the corporate signatories to commit to increasing diversity in their own law departments as well as in the law firms that they engaged as outside counsel. "Call to Action" was a highly visible catalyst for change in corporate law departments throughout the country for many years. However, the commitment to diversity appears to be leveling off, as evidenced by the some of the findings of our current study.

---

[10] A Call to Action—Diversity in the Legal Profession (available at http://www.acc.com/vl/public/Article/loader.cfm?csModule=security/getfile&pageid=16074). See also http://www.generalmills.com/Company/Leadership/Roderick_Rick_A_Palmore.aspx; Stephanie Francis Ward, Rick Palmore: Demanding Diversity, ABA Journal (http://www.abajournal.com/legalrebels/article/demanding_diversity).

Studies demonstrate that organizations that embrace diversity achieve greater success.[11] To attract and retain the best and the brightest legal talent, and enhance opportunities for the greatest success, corporate law departments (and law firms) must work to reduce attrition and promote the career satisfaction of all lawyers. The recommendations that follow address the concerns respondents raised in the Commission's study on women of color in Fortune 500 law departments and provide strategies that will help ensure the success of this group of attorneys well into the future.

Recommendations

In Visible Invisibility, its study of women of color in law firms, the Commission proffered the following solutions to assist law firms in integrating women of color into existing diversity, retention, and professional development efforts:

- Address the success of women of color as a firm issue.
- Integrate women of color into existing measurement efforts.
- Integrate women of color into the firm's professional fabric.
- Integrate women of color into the firm's social fabric.
- Increase awareness of issues of women of color through dialogue.
- Support women of color's efforts to build internal and external support systems.
- Comply with anti-discrimination and anti-harassment policies and hold people accountable for noncompliance.[12]

These suggested strategies are just as relevant now as they were then and apply equally to corporate law departments. Fortune 500 companies are encouraged to review and incorporate these suggestions into their existing diversity programming. In addition to these strategies, the Commission offers the following recommendations to the leadership of corporate legal

---

[11] E.g., McKinsey & Co., Women Matter: Gender Diversity, A Corporate Performance Driver (Oct. 2007); see also McKinsey & Co., Women Matter 2010: Women at the Top of Corporations: Making It Happen (Oct. 2010) (both available at http://www.mckinsey.com/client_service/organization/latest_thinking/women_matter).

[12] Visible Invisibility, supra note 2, at 37-40.

departments as a result of its work on this phase of its Women of Color Research Initiative.

Overall

<u>Formulate and implement a comprehensive diversity and retention plan.</u>

- Involve leaders at top levels of the company in developing a comprehensive plan that integrates diversity and inclusion into all aspects of the department's functions by using metrics to create a baseline and implement programs designed to stem attrition and foster teamwork and inclusion.
- Integrate the ability to develop and advance all groups of people as a leadership competency.
- Task department leaders with developing a plan for creation of affinity groups, a key to a comprehensive diversity and retention plan. Such affinity groups can include women of color from both the legal and business sides of the organization. The support and camaraderie that affinity groups offer can help to counter the feelings of isolation and marginalization reported by many women in both law firms and corporate law departments.
- Use affinity groups to foster networking, and provide a forum for professional development, educational services and training, community outreach, and mentoring to its members, as well as to identify challenges in the culture of the organization.

<u>Actively communicate the notion that diversity breeds excellence and that the two are not mutually exclusive concepts.</u>

- Communicate to all members of the legal department through its mission statements and formal diversity policies that diversity, done right, breeds excellence by bringing together the best and brightest from all demographic groups.
- Nip concerns about reverse discrimination in the bud. Underlying such concerns is the assumption that the women and minorities are inherently unqualified—and that every white male is qualified. Through consistent messaging about the value of diversity and

visible action in furtherance of inclusive policies, law departments can move the reverse discrimination issue from a discussion of exclusion to one of inclusion.

- Hold department leaders accountable for ensuring diversity of their legal teams, as well as for their outside counsel.
- Identify ways to integrate diversity into ongoing discussions of departmental excellence and employee engagement.

Hiring and Recruitment

<u>Develop a comprehensive plan for recruiting and hiring a diverse staff to make maximum use of the talent pool.</u>

- Leverage women's and minority-based affinity groups and bar associations to recruit diverse candidates.
- Strengthen ties with law school administration, faculty, and student organizations, and increase the amount of time and resources allotted to on-campus interviews, given that female attorneys of color appear to rely more heavily on law school-related resources than other groups to secure their first in-house job.
- Broaden the pipeline to include high potential applicants from law schools with a high proportion of minorities and women.
- Use minority student organizations, such as the Black Law Student Association, Hispanic Law Student Association, and the Asian/Pacific American Law Student Association, as on-campus resources of diverse talent.
- Increase outreach through job-posting and other opportunities on national and local bars with a focus on diverse attorneys.
- Conduct outreach at specialty bar associations and diversity focused events.

Retention

<u>Offer regular and meaningful opportunities for law department members to work and socialize across racial, ethnic, gender, and generational boundaries.</u>

- Encourage development of informal relationships and mentorship opportunities by providing regular and ongoing opportunities for law department members to interact both on a department-wide basis and in smaller practice-based groups and to interact with clients on the business side of the company. Social interaction can take a variety of forms, ranging from formal breakfasts, luncheons, and dinners to informal "meet-and-greets," team-building activities, and law department gatherings for members' families.

- Encourage senior law department members to drop by the offices of their women of color colleagues to ask how they are doing and to offer assistance, if needed.
- Establish and use affinity groups to help train and educate existing staff on diversity issues and cultural sensitivity.
- Identify ways in which leaders can be held accountable for giving adequate and effective feedback to women of color.

Develop a consistent, top-down, zero-tolerance policy toward acts of workplace bias against women of color, both subtle and overt, and be prepared to have hard conversations with staff regarding expectations of fairness and accountability.

- Develop an accessible, yet confidential, reporting structure through which violations of anti-bias policies can be communicated and investigated. Women of color must feel comfortable in reporting acts of bias without fear of retaliation or negative repercussion on their careers.
- Identify clearly defined consequences for the violations of these policies that are applicable to every member of the law department regardless of where they fall in the hierarchy. An anti-bias policy is only as strong as its enforcement.

Develop effective work-life balance and integration programs.

- There is often a stigma associated with the use of work-life balance/integration programs, especially for female attorneys. For such programs to be utilized and effective, legal employers must ensure that these programs are stigma-free and gender neutral.

Develop policies that ensure that all members of the legal department have equal access to information and resources.

- Female attorneys of color often lack access to informal mentors and networks that provide valuable information and opportunities for advancement, including good work assignments, which can make a tremendous difference in whether the attorney ultimately achieves success. As such, it is imperative that deliberate measures be taken to ensure that all legal department members are included and involved in activities that are valued and accessible by all.

- All female attorneys should have equal access to the tools and information necessary to perform her job and thus achieve success.

Develop systems that review assignments and ensure that all attorneys are receiving access to high quality assignments and training.

- Access to high quality work assignments is the lifeblood for a successful career as a lawyer. However, due in large part to unintentional bias, access is often based on whom the assigner knows or is comfortable with—usually another male attorney. In this way, it is imperative that department leaders develop more equitable and objective mechanisms for disseminating and reviewing work assignments across their legal teams.

- The source of work assignments is also important. Assignments from influential individuals often provide higher visibility and the most gains.

- Efforts should be made to ensure that all attorneys receive similar training opportunities on legal, business, and other issues important to the company.

Provide ongoing education and training on cultural disparities and sensitivities, particularly those affecting women of color.

- Engage in ongoing education and training on issues of bias, especially unconscious bias. The goal is to create a common ground of understanding through dialogue and shared experience.

- Provide training to all employees on subconscious bias and stereotyping and the importance of an inclusive workplace to the success of the company.

Advancement

<u>Develop transparent, bias-free performance evaluation systems, and clearly communicate benchmarks and performance standards to all members of the legal department.</u>

- Develop and monitor metrics to measure success in improving retention and diversity.
- Appoint a representative team to design and implement a bias-free evaluation process.

    o Develop job descriptions and objectives that identify the knowledge, skills, and abilities necessary for each class or job level.
    o Develop job-related competencies.
    o Implement an attorney self-evaluation process.
    o Implement an upward review process to help identify possible biases or tendencies that might indicate unconscious bias or exclusion. For example, does a senior lawyer have lunch only with people of his or her gender or race?

- Establish and publish a bias-free performance evaluation policy and process.

    o Establish how often the formal evaluation process will be conducted.
    o Educate the department about the policy through department-wide meetings.
    o Obtain buy-in by stressing the benefits of this policy and connecting it to department or company objectives and its cost savings as a result of lower attrition and greater employee satisfaction.
    o Work with mentors to implement the policy and evaluation process.

- Train personnel about how to conduct bias-free evaluations.
- Review evaluation forms to identify unconscious bias. For example, do comments reflect gender bias or leniency bias, which rates

certain lawyers higher than their performance would indicate is appropriate or that assumes that a man's mistakes are evidence of potential but a woman's errors of the same type mean that she is not capable?

- Encourage informal feedback on a regular basis, outside of the formal evaluation process.
- Provide constructive feedback on performance and training and advice on how to improve performance and bolster areas where additional expertise is warranted.

Develop transparent strategies for equitable succession planning.

- Develop criteria for making decisions about who will succeed retiring attorneys or upper level attorneys who leave the law department to help ensure that such decisions are made fairly, that all qualified candidates are given equal consideration, and that decisions are not made based on personal relationships or without consideration of diversity and objective factors.
- Develop a process and objective factors to ensure that female attorneys of color are afforded the same critical developmental opportunities as lawyers in other groups that will groom them for leadership. This requires a more strategic approach of viewing their career progression as a series of incremental steps toward a particular career-related goal (i.e., general counsel) to ensure that each step or rung of the ladder prepares them adequately for the next phase.

Compensation

Implement processes that ensure that compensation decisions are made fairly and with transparency.

- Appoint compensation committees that reflect the diversity of the department and its commitment to diversity.
- Compare compensation, including salary, bonuses, options, and benefits, across all demographic groups in the department. Use these statistics to create a baseline and measure progress toward equalizing pay for comparable work year on year.

- Use objective metrics to help ensure that all attorneys in a certain class or level are paid equally for comparable work, regardless of race, ethnicity, or gender.
- Eliminate organizational structures and policies that may unintentionally disadvantage female attorneys of color (e.g., focus on actual performance, not how and where the work is performed, etc.).

Reprinted with permission from the American Bar Association

ASPATORE